The Development of the
Peace Idea

Benjamin F. Trueblood

THE DEVELOPMENT OF THE PEACE IDEA
AND OTHER ESSAYS

BY

BENJAMIN F. TRUEBLOOD, LL.D.

Author of *The Federation of the World*

COLLECTED AND NEWLY ISSUED

INTRODUCTION BY EDWIN D. MEAD

BOSTON, 1932

PRINTED IN THE UNITED STATES OF AMERICA
BY THE PLIMPTON PRESS · NORWOOD · MASS.

To

THE COLLEAGUES AND FRIENDS

OF

BENJAMIN F. TRUEBLOOD

IN AMERICA AND EUROPE

AND TO

THE FRIENDS OF PEACE

EVERYWHERE

PREFATORY NOTE

THAT there is still need for our father's message prompts us to bring together certain of his occasional writings. They seem singularly modern and applicable, even after decades have intervened, and although the peace movement has developed and deepened much as he foresaw it would. The World War only added point to his conclusions and gave further historical evidence of the need for world federation.

We have chosen papers that together present a somewhat connected study of the development of the peace idea. In busy years as Secretary of the American Peace Society, 1892 to 1915, the writer of these essays so devoted himself to addresses and lectures and to making the *Advocate of Peace* an effective medium for the expression of his thought that he spared little time for treatises or studies in the form of books; but since his death it has seemed to his family there should be a collected edition such as this to bear witness to his teaching and perhaps give it a wider hearing.

To the memory of his brave and sacrificial life we dedicate this little volume.

L. T. W.
F. T. S.

CONTENTS

Pax Quaerenda Pace

INTRODUCTION

THE peace movement as a definite and organized movement began in the United States, in 1815. During the centuries great peace prophets, Dante, Erasmus, Grotius, William Penn, Rousseau, Immanuel Kant, and other glorious pioneers had risen in long and noble apostolic succession to denounce the war system and demand a just and ordered international life. But the first peace society in the world was the New York Peace Society, founded by David Low Dodge in August, 1815, two months after Waterloo. In Christmas week of the same year, the Massachusetts Peace Society was founded by Noah Worcester and William Ellery Channing. The English Peace Society, organized in London, in 1816, was the first in Europe. The Massachusetts Peace Society rapidly became large and influential; and local societies multiplied in various parts of the country. In 1828, mainly through the efforts of William Ladd, who had left his beloved Maine farm for his consecrated and untiring missionary life in the high cause, the American Peace Society was established, by the federation of the local societies. Ladd became the chairman of its Board of Directors and its secretary; and he was the dominant figure in the American peace cause to the time of his death, in 1841. The various local societies had had various principles and conditions of membership, the early New York Peace Society prescribing that its members must be members of the Church; but the American Peace Society, in its statement of principles in 1828, declared: "We receive into our communion all who seek to abolish war."

The American Peace Society had several secretaries between William Ladd and Benjamin Franklin Trueblood; but only one of them stands out conspicuously. George Cone Beckwith was secretary of the Society from 1837 to 1870, a full generation, a period, too, crowded with events of great moment to the cause. Ladd, Beckwith, and Trueblood were successively identified with the developments which marked the progress of the American peace movement.

William Ladd is a classic and heroic figure in the history of the American Peace Society. His devotion and his untiring labors for the cause of peace were like those of Wesley in the cause of Methodism. He persisted in his unyielding crusade until he was so feeble that he had to sit in the pulpit of the churches where he spoke. "Why should I be unwilling to risk my life in the cause?" He died the day after addressing a great audience in Boston. Yet more impressive, if possible, than Ladd's consecration was his vision. He had the true philosophy of the peace movement. He knew that peace could come only through adequate world organization. There must be a federation of nations, as our orderly republic was constituted through the federation of our states. His famous essay on "A Congress of Nations," published in 1840, although some of its principles had been anticipated by Worcester and others, marked an epoch. It urged not only a Congress of Nations, but a Court of Nations, to arbitrate cases brought before it by contending parties. Dr. James Brown Scott has said that Ladd's plan was essentially realized in the Hague Conference of 1899 and the resulting tribunal. Elihu Burritt truly said that Ladd was the first to give an American shaping to the idea of an international assembly. John Quincy Adams was so impressed by the force of Ladd's reasoning that he declared optimistically that the project would be realized within twenty years. It made a profound impression not only in America but all over the world. Ten thousand copies were circulated in England alone.

Ladd's principles were the central principles of the American delegates to the great International Peace Congresses at Brussels, Paris, Frankfort, and London, from 1848 to 1851, the most famous and perhaps the most influential of all peace congresses.

These were projected in the office of the American
Peace Society in Boston; and Elihu Burritt was
their chief inspirer and organizer. His addresses and
those of his associates at those Congresses made a
profound impression by their definiteness and con-
structiveness; and the policy of working for peace
through the creation of an International Congress
and Court was spoken of throughout Europe as
"the American way." It was the plan for which
Woodrow Wilson and Elihu Root have labored in
this time in the League of Nations and the World
Court. It is one of the most amazing and mournful
ironies of history that in this critical period of
reconstruction following the World War "the
American way" should, through the vicissitudes of
our party politics, have been adopted by every civilized power except ourselves and that the American
republic alone still stands outside the organized
family of nations.

Beckwith's secretaryship of the American Peace
Society, thirty-three years, covered the whole period
of these great international peace congresses, the
trying period of the Mexican War and of the Civil
War. Almost his whole working life was given to
the great cause to which he was so deeply devoted.

The early days of the American Peace Society
were days of hardship and struggle, often of un-
popularity, with heroic, underpaid, self-sacrificing

officials. The support came chiefly from New England, New York, and Pennsylvania. When Ladd in his crusade for the organizing of the American Peace Society went to New York, the largest of his five audiences numbered five persons. The annual income of the Society during its first four years was less than four hundred dollars. The receipts of the early Massachusetts Peace Society in its most flourishing days had not exceeded one thousand dollars a year. Noah Worcester often lived on bread and water and made his own shoes in order to put his meager earnings as preacher into the cause to which his life was devoted. The achievements of these early men, the founders of our American Peace movement, were prodigious; in view of their slight resources they were almost incredible. The myriad meetings which they held, the numberless pamphlets which they circulated, the branches which they established up and down the land, the congresses which they prompted and prepared, fill us with amazement and in our easier days put us to shame. They witness to the mighty power of high purpose, of careful study, of commanding conviction, and of a definite program. It is well for us in this day of peace foundations and endowments with their millions to remember this heroism and hardship of the fathers of the movement. Dr. Trueblood never forgot them; and had it been necessary to resort to bread and water to keep the work going, he would not have shrunk from it, for he was of that stuff.

William Ladd was the first president of the American Peace Society, the first five years of Beckwith's secretaryship. For ten years of Beckwith's service, 1848 to 1858, the president was William Jay, who published a powerful arraignment of our wanton war with Mexico. The president from 1891 to 1910, covering the greater part of Dr. Trueblood's administration as secretary, was Robert Treat Paine. During his last years the president was Theodore E. Burton. There were a dozen other presidents but these are the outstanding men, as Ladd, Beckwith, and Trueblood were the outstanding secretaries. It was doubtless Mr. Paine who, the year after he became president, secured Dr. Trueblood's services and brought him to Boston. The relations of the two men were singularly coöperative, cordial, and affectionate. Mr. Paine, a grandson of the Robert Treat Paine who signed the Declaration of Independence, a Harvard scholar, a close friend of Phillips Brooks, identified with the leading social and philanthropic activities of the city, was a Bostonian of the Bostonians. Dr. Trueblood was a western man, the first western man who had held conspicuous place in the administration of the Peace Society, which had been almost exclusively in the hands of New Englanders and New Yorkers.

They were both tall men, six-footers, of imposing presence, and during their joint administration the Peace Society certainly had a commanding front. Mr. Paine well knew Dr. Trueblood's superior knowledge and experience in the movement, and his deference and loyalty to his administration were always signal.

Only by reviewing the peace movement in America before 1892 can one understand Dr. Trueblood's service and his place in the movement. His place was that of the bridge between the old peace movement and the new. He was the one conspicuous and representative worker who stood with one foot in the period before the Hague Conferences and with the other in the period of the World War which resulted in the League of Nations. No other among us understood that history so well; and no other was so conscious of the inspiring and shaping relations of the past to the present. He never permitted his associates to forget the historical background; and he would not wish us to pay tribute to his contributions without pious and intelligent recognition of his inheritance.

Benjamin Franklin Trueblood was born in Salem, Indiana, in 1847, and died in Newton, Massachusetts, in 1916. Salem means Peace; and in this same Salem nine years before was born John Hay, destined to be the great Peace Secretary of

State. By eloquent coincidence the two men were together on the platform of Tremont Temple in Boston at the opening session of the great International Peace Congress of 1904; one who gave the chief address on that occasion as Secretary of State, the other as Secretary of the American Peace Society. Benjamin Trueblood's parents were members of the Society of Friends; and there was in the town a little peace society. The boy studied at Earlham College in Indiana, a Friends college, graduating in 1869; then he studied theology and taught school; and presently he became professor of Greek and Latin at Penn College in Iowa, another Friends college. In 1874 he was called to the presidency of Wilmington College in Ohio, having meantime taken an Ohio wife; and for five years he remained in Wilmington, which ever had a tender place in his affection. There his first child died; and there his own body was borne for its final rest, in the autumn of 1916. From Wilmington College he went back to Penn College as its president until 1890, and after a year in Europe in the service of the Christian Arbitration and Peace Society of Philadelphia, he came in January, 1892, to the secretaryship of the American Peace Society in Boston, which was to prove the great work of his life. He never quite outgrew the feeling of the college professor or indeed of the college student. He liked the society of young men, and young men liked him. I once went out with him from Boston — I was for some years a Director of the American Peace Society — to an Intercollegiate Peace Congress at his old Earlham College. We were there for three days, sleeping in the dormitory, having our meals with the students in the common room. Half the professors were his friends, and their welcome was warm, but he was happier with the students even than with their teachers, a jovial boy again in the old places. When the Cosmopolitan Clubs sprang up in our colleges and universities twenty-five years ago, nobody welcomed the movement more warmly than he or was more quickly taken into confidence and conference by the young men; he was invited as the chief speaker to two or three of the early national conventions.

We thus see that Benjamin Trueblood was essentially an academic man, a scholar. He was the best scholar who had ever been related officially to the American Peace Society, and one of the greatest scholars associated with the peace cause in America. He had been a Greek and Latin professor; he made an admirable translation of Kant's " Zum Ewigen Frieden "; and he made easy use of French and Italian. He was a life-long student of philosophy and theology, of history and politics. A ready and impressive speaker, he gave innumerable addresses for the peace cause all over the country. A cogent writer and a good editor, he made the Advocate of Peace, the organ of the Peace Society, for a long period the best international journal in the world. There was never cotton-wool in his mouth, nor mud in his ink. He had knowledge, he had conviction, he had definiteness of purpose, and he always shot at a mark.

When Dr. Trueblood began his service as secretary of the American Peace Society in 1892, and for many years afterwards, it is right to say that he was the only professional peace worker in the United States, the only man who made service of the peace cause his vocation. Today, with the foundations and associations of various character, there are scores of salaried men and women devoting their lives to the work. In Dr. Trueblood's early days in Boston he stood alone; it may almost be said that he was the organized peace movement in America, so far as vocation was concerned. There were sundry peace societies in the country, mainly religious, and mostly feeble; but the American Peace Society was essentially the American peace movement, and Dr. Trueblood was its active head and hand. Loyal and loving helpers he had. To one of these, Charles E. Beals, for a time in the Boston office, then the head of the Chicago department, all friends of the peace cause are grateful for the sympathetic and careful paper on Dr. Trueblood's life and work which he prepared at the time of his death.

In 1911 the headquarters of the Peace Society were removed from Boston to Washington. Dr. Trueblood felt that this would emphasize the Society's national function and character, and that at the capital it could exercise a stronger political influence; and the new World Peace Foundation, established and generously endowed by Edwin Ginn, would keep the cause well represented in Boston. Yet the Peace Society did not desert Boston. Once more a Massachusetts Peace Society was organized, in affiliation with Washington, and at the same time department centres were established in New York and Chicago, in the South and on the Pacific Coast. With failing health in his last years, Dr. Trueblood remained in Washington until a year before his death when he returned to his old home in Newton.

Born into a Quaker home, he always remained a loyal Quaker. Brother of every religious man, working harmoniously with all, the Quaker principles and spirit and traditions were very dear to him. He revered the memory of George Fox; Whittier was pre-eminently his poet; and he was a lifelong and profound student of William Penn. There was ever something of the Quaker simplicity

and directness about him. His communication was
Yea and Nay. He was often severe, a man of great
dignity, but never stern, and he had an unfailing
strain of humor; he enjoyed a laugh; and upon
rare occasions burst over into what John Hay would
call "huge mirth," the term which Hay does apply
to another's robust merriment. He had plenty of
occasion for mirth, and for some sarcasm. He dis-
liked sentimentality and ineptitude; and the peace
cause, like every great cause, has never been without its cranks and bores, men in its counsels and
conferences of the sort of whom Emerson in the
anti-slavery time spoke as "fleas of conventions."
He had good red-blooded wrath, and sundry per-
formances in the Senate during these last years
would have drawn his lightning. When the Senate
rejected the Olney-Pauncefote treaty in 1897, he
exclaimed, "One is justified in following the example of the archangel Michael in disputing with
the Devil about the body of Moses, and saying,
'The Lord rebuke thee, O Senate.'"

With the organized peace movement in Europe
Dr. Trueblood was for a decade almost our sole
link. The International Peace Congresses were
revived in 1889. He was not present at the Congress
in Paris that year, but he was at London in 1890,
and from then to the Geneva Congress in 1912
there were few sessions which he missed. There

were two sessions in the United States, at Chicago in 1893 and at Boston in 1904. The Chicago Congress was in the year following his entrance upon the secretaryship of the American Peace Society, and it was almost entirely arranged and managed by him. He was long the only American representative on the International Peace Bureau. He was at The Hague during the First Hague Conference in 1899. He took active part in all the national peace congresses in the United States, which beginning with the great New York Congress of 1907 continued until the St. Louis Congress of 1913, the year before the World War.

The period of Dr. Trueblood's service as secretary of the American Peace Society was almost exactly covered by the series of annual conferences on international arbitration at Lake Mohonk. The first of these Mohonk Conferences was in 1895 and they continued until 1916; and during those twenty-two years few peace agencies in the country exercised a more marked influence; no other organization assembled so important a body of peace leaders, and none more definitely affected our international policies. At nearly all of these Mohonk Conferences Dr. Trueblood was present and influential; and almost always he presented at the opening session a careful survey of the world's international activities during the preceding year as a basis for proceedings. There was no other man in the country then to whom such a service so fittingly fell; there were few others who had the varied and thorough information which qualified them for its discharge. A collection of those old surveys would present comprehensively the problems and progress of the peace movement during that period. His mind was constructive. His sobriety and statesmanship commanded respect; and he had significant conferences with Presidents McKinley, Roosevelt, Taft, and Wilson at critical times on questions of public policy. A rightly organized world was his primary concern; but he never ceased to demand that preparations for war should be cut precisely as preparations for order and peace advanced. The monstrous armaments themselves are occasions and provocations of war. As an early member of the American Society of International Law, he wrote for its journal a strong article on " The Case for Limitation of Armaments," and in his addresses and his editorials he fought constantly the big navy craze.

Scholar that he was, Dr. Trueblood was first and foremost a crusader, fighting the battles of the day; and his weapons had to be speeches and pamphlets and not books. In 1898 he published his valuable volume on " The Federation of the World," one of the best reviews that had ever

been prepared of the steps and the strivings toward
world organization up to the years before the first
Hague Conference. Now, fifteen years after his
death, several of his essays and addresses have been
brought together for this volume. Some were
printed in the Advocate of Peace, and others are
from the store of his papers, reflecting his later
work. The collection will be welcomed not only for
its intrinsic worth, but also as a grateful memorial
of a life and work which the friends of peace will
not permit to be forgotten.

Dr. Trueblood was always optimistic and he
believed that a reliable principle of progress informs
history. He had bitter disappointments, worst of all
the World War, which shocked him as the kind of
catastrophe which he believed Christendom had outgrown; and in it he could do nothing. But this is
God's world, he held stoutly, and despite every
setback and defeat God's Kingdom would surely be
established on earth. The first words of his first
editorial in the Advocate of Peace, in 1892, were
a quotation from John Wesley, "God buries the
workmen, but carries forward the work."

In this spirit we contemplate his brave, persistent,
and constructive life. It touched the day of small
things in the peace movement, the potential things
and men whom he taught us so well how to appreciate and to revere; and it saw the dawn of the

larger things which we see and share. Other men
have labored and we enter into the fruits of their
labors. Let not the children forget the fathers.
Dodge, Worcester, Channing, Ladd, Burritt,
Sumner — these were a great generation in the
peace movement in America. So in the world was
the generation which numbered Hodgson Pratt,
Darby, Cremer, and Moscheles in England,
Frédéric Passy in France, La Fontaine in Belgium,
Bajer in Denmark, Moneta in Italy, Ducommun
at Berne, Richter and Quidde in Germany, the
Baroness von Suttner and Alfred Fried at Vienna.
All of these were Benjamin Trueblood's friends
and fellow-workers; among them all there was no
more clairvoyant, consecrated, or confident soul
than he.

EDWIN D. MEAD

THE
HISTORIC DEVELOPMENT
OF THE PEACE IDEA [1]

PEACE is not only a fundamental doctrine of Christianity, it is equally a fundamental doctrine of
humanity in its essential constitution. Hence peace,
both as an idea and as a social attainment, has had a
natural historic development, in which other forces
than Christian teaching, or any other religious teaching, technically such, have played a powerful and
incessant part. These natural forces began to act
earlier, perhaps, than the religious, and though de-
pendent on the religious for their vitalization, they
seem to have acted more steadily than the latter.

The religious conception of peace as a moral demand, though in its use by religious teachers it has
had a very fluctuating history, has nevertheless since
the time of Christ led the whole historic development
of the peace movement. It has been a sort of head-
master to the movement, giving to it now and then

---

[1] A paper read at the Haverford, Pa., Summer School of
Religious History, June, 1900; subsequently revised and
printed in the *Advocate of Peace*, and as a pamphlet.

impulse, inspiration and direction, and stirring the natural peace forces into stronger and more effective activity. It is only as the religious and the natural phases of the movement are both taken into account that the historic development of the principle and practice of peace can be properly understood.

The idea of peace as a matter of moral obligation and the practical application of pacific methods in social and international affairs have developed at about the same rate. The growth and extension of the idea can therefore be fairly well traced in terms of its practical application in conciliation, mediation, arbitration, and the evolution of law and order in society.

UNKNOWN TO THE ANCIENT WORLD

The idea of universal and perpetual peace, which has taken such a wide and deep hold upon the thought of recent times, was unknown to the ancient world. The controlling principle among all the ancient peoples as to peace and war was that of family or race. Within a patriarchal group, a tribe, or collection of tribes within a common race, the idea of peace as useful and even obligatory was usually considerably developed. This is the case now among the unchristianized peoples of the world. Tribes which fight like fiends with one another manage, in spite of their ignorance, unrestraint and animalism, to keep up within themselves a fair amount of friendship and pacific life and coöperation.

The forces which operated among the ancient peoples in producing this measure of pacific life were sense of kinship, contiguity of dwelling, interdependence and some realized community of interests. Beyond this sphere of race or family, war, pillage, conquest, enslavement, were considered not only permissible but also obligatory. Often the obligations of peace were felt only within very narrow limits, the tendency being, until Christianity began to operate, to reduce the feeling of obligation to the minimum of family relationship rather than to expand it to the limits of racial kinship.

The religions of the ancient peoples, growing as they did largely out of the characters of the peoples and their environments, deepened and strengthened these conceptions. The national gods were looked upon as protecting and favoring the home people, but as hostile to all others. Where strange gods were brought in and domesticated, the purpose was probably nearly always to secure the most help in war or the greatest security against hostile inroads from without. The principal use of gods was for war purposes.

THE JEWISH CONCEPTION OF PEACE

The same principle of race governed the Jewish people in the matter of peace and war. The peace for which their psalmists and prophets sighed was peace upon Israel, the peace of Jerusalem, not the peace of the world, of nation with nation. War against heathen peoples was considered not only lawful but obligatory. Love of other peoples and rational treatment of them was scarcely dreamed of amongst the Hebrews. Love of neighbor was as far as they got, and their theory of this was much better than their practice. In their conception of God, in regard to some of his attributes, they rose, or were lifted, vastly higher than any other nation of their time. Their God, the one true and living God, was the creator of all nations and peoples, as well as of the heavens and of the earth. But it is curious that this conception of God never led them to see and feel the real kinship and oneness of humanity, as one might expect it would have done. They drew from it rather the selfish notion of great superiority over other peoples. They believed that this God, their God, meant them to bring all other nations under their sway, and that the Messiah whom he was to send would do this service for them. Not even their greatest prophets were able wholly to divest themselves of the racial narrowness of view. They now

and then, as in the case of Isaiah, Micah, Ezekiel,
Zechariah, had glimpses of the larger peace of the
world, but its true nature and method of attainment
they failed to grasp. It was to come by their God
rebuking the other nations and causing them to flow
to the mountain of the Lord, the house of the God
of Jacob. It was in the holy mountain of Israel that
the lamb and the lion were to lie down together,
and the cow and the bear to feed in friendship. The
larger meaning which we see in the prophetic peace
passages was in them, but it was not the prophets
themselves who put it there, or who even understood that it was there. It was not until Jesus Christ
had unfolded the idea of the universal brotherhood
of men as the corollary of the Fatherhood of God
that any Jew was able to see " the middle wall of
partition " broken down and to comprehend the
true basis of a universal peace founded on the equal
rights of all men and all nations.

AMONG THE GREEKS AND ROMANS

The nearest approach to modern peace conceptions, outside of two or three of the Jewish prophets
and rabbis, was found among the Greek philosophers
and poets. There was something of this nature in
both Confucius and Buddha, but it is doubtful if
the " universal benevolence " of the one or the
" fraternity of humanity " of the other went beyond

the great races to which they belonged. Their teachings certainly had no social effect in the relations of these peoples to others. Pride of race and contempt of other peoples have not been deeper anywhere else than in India and China. The reputed peaceful character of the Chinese, among whom the soldier has held a place very inferior to that of the scholar, has been due in part to sluggishness and immobility, and not largely to active love and benevolence, or even to pacific instincts.

Greece, though a small country, came into close touch with a number of nations. Her sages therefore — Socrates, Plato, Democritus, Diogenes, Theodorus and later ones — had a larger and truer conception of humanity and a deeper perception of the need of peace than was found elsewhere. But still the teachings of these sages had no discoverable effect on the relations of the Greek people to others. The Greek mind in general, in its pride of race, seemed incapable of grasping — at any rate it was unwilling to grasp — the idea of a common universal humanity. In the case of the sages themselves this conception seems to have been rather a pleasurable picture of the imagination than a commanding ethical idea. " The world is my country," a saying attributed to Socrates, meant in the mouth of a Greek, at home or in exile, not that the citizens of other countries were his equals and brethren, but that he as a superior being had a right to stride abroad wherever he pleased, and that all others ought to accept and treat him as such. However, there was among the best of the Greeks, as among the most spiritual of the Hebrew prophets, some partially developed consciousness of the common humanity.

Among Roman thinkers there was something of the larger peace conception found among the wise men of Greece. But this was in large measure an imitation of Greek thought, and was therefore fruitless for good. The general idea of peace among the Romans, the *pax Romana*, was wholly a political conception, being expressive of the relations of the parts of the empire to one another and to the overlord at Rome. It was, however, not wholly without moral quality. It is impossible to keep this quality out of the relations of men, even though their conduct towards one another be in considerable measure dictated by a superior. The adjudications — they can hardly be called arbitrations — between various subject states of the Roman empire, made by the emperor or his subordinates, trained these peoples in self-restraint, in resort to reason, and in the use of pacific methods. Thus, in spite of the fact that the Roman empire was a huge system of political slavery, a real contribution was made to the development of the peace idea through the practical use of pacific methods.

ARBITRATION LITTLE KNOWN IN THE ANCIENT WORLD

In general, in the ancient world, the use of pacific methods of settling disputes was as limited as the idea of peace. In the case of Rome, as we have just seen, it was purely internal and political. Rome never arbitrated with other nations, or acted as arbitrator for them. When two contending states appealed to her, she ended the controversy as the judge did that about the oyster. She ate the oyster; she annexed the states. Among other peoples the use of conciliation or arbitration was purely a family or race affair. The herdsmen of Lot and of Abraham were to cease their strife because they were brethren. The herdsmen of either might fight those of an outsider as much as they liked, when it was safe or expedient to do so. The Amphictyonic councils among the Greeks were family tribunals, set up for the purpose of adjusting differences and preventing war among brethren, among peoples of kindred blood. Greece as a whole, or even in parts, did not arbitrate with outside nations. The arbitration of the dispute between the two sons of Darius as to which should have the throne, referred to their uncle and decided by him, was still more of this domestic type.

Beyond this limited racial sphere the idea of peace

(except in the case of a few prophets and sages) and the practical application of peace methods never went, in pre-Christian times. There does not seem to have been any tendency, so far as can be traced, to anything of a wider and more universal nature, to anything of a truly international character. Even within this limited sphere the practical pacific effects of the sense of kinship were very small. The principle of kinship, though lying at the basis of the whole pacific development of human society, was not naturally strong enough to accomplish much anywhere until it was elevated, purified and strengthened by the revelation of the fact that it is not of merely earthly origin, but is rooted in the divine Fatherhood in which alone the oneness of humanity finds its rational explanation.

THE CONCEPTION GIVEN BY JESUS AND HIS FOLLOWERS

The true and complete conception of peace, both as to its motives and its scope, was given to the world for the first time by Jesus Christ and his early followers. They taught such doctrines of God as the Father and of men everywhere as brothers and neighbors as naturally broke down among the Christians, after a little time, racial distinctions and international barriers. Perhaps practised would be a better word than taught. Love of God and of fellow-men was their life. Jesus himself gave the

idea of peace in its deepest and fullest sense. But he
did more; he made it intensely vital by his life of
self-sacrificing love. His teaching came out of his
life. The inspiration of his example, of his life and
death, was worth a thousand Sermons-on-the-
Mount, unsurpassed as the mountain instruction
was. The Sermon on the Mount does not seem to
have been much used in the earliest Christian days,
though after the New Testament books were
written and collected it had a large place. In the
earliest period it was entirely overshadowed by the
Teacher himself. It was the inspiration of his personality, of his living example, the transfusing of his
personal spirit into them, that made the early Christians, for a hundred years and more, the enthusiastic
exemplars of a fraternity which knew neither class
nor race nor national boundaries. Followers of the
Master in every land recognized their spiritual kin,
and their human kin also, in every other land. Their
homes, their purses, their lives, were at each other's
service. War between them, or between them and
non-Christians, was unthinkable. It will be so again
when the Christian Church once more becomes
really Christian. International and inter-racial
hatred between them was even more completely
broken down than local dislike and friction. Among
themselves difficulties, of which there were many,
were settled by conciliation or the arbitration of

friends, not even the courts of law being often resorted to. Thus came into existence the conception of universal peace as the demand of universal brotherhood and universal love.

HAD AT FIRST LITTLE SOCIAL EFFECT

It is a disappointing fact that early Christianity, during the whole of this wonderful period, pure and fresh and masterful as it was, working its way with marvellous rapidity into all lands, had practically no pacific social effect beyond its own circles. Its current ran within itself. The nations in their relations to each other were untouched by it. They despised each other and fought on as before. Where Rome ruled, the *pax Romana* was all the international peace that was known. Among other peoples the idea of race or family still controlled.

The cause of this failure of Christianity to produce any pacific effect outside of its own borders, if failure it may be called, was that the kingdom of heaven was conceived as something beyond this world and its affairs, with which it was thought that Christians should have little to do. Terrestrial affairs were to be wound up soon, by the early return of the Lord. No effort was made, therefore, to bring Christianity to bear upon existing political institutions. Perhaps none was possible under the circumstances of the times.

From the opening of the fourth century, Christianity, when it had become popular and was in a position to begin to control general social and international relations, fell away from its previous spirit and practice. Christian men went to war alongside unchristian men. They fell into the narrow patriotism which prevailed. The high ideal of Jesus and his early followers gradually passed out of sight. Their doctrine of universal brotherhood gave way in practice to the old notion of race or family kinship and superiority, a principle which, narrowly and selfishly used, has probably caused almost half the mischief ever done. Thus the Christian practice of peace and opposition to the whole business of war, which seemed on the point of mastering the world, ceased in large measure.

LONG PERIOD OF DARKNESS

There follows a long period of darkness, extending to and overlapping the Reformation, in which humanity touched about as low depths of division and strife as it ever reached. The *pax Romana*, the peace of dominion, of political slavery, continued in measure until the fall of the empire. When this was destroyed during the fierce struggles of the barbarian invasions, Europe was broken up, and the efforts to restore the empire succeeded only for brief periods. During the confusion which followed and the period of the feudal lordships, both public and private war were well-nigh incessant. This period includes the long struggle of the papacy for universal political dominion. It was the period of the "holy wars," when Christianity itself was perverted into an instrument of cruelty and bloodshed.

It must not be inferred that during this long period of twelve hundred years Christianity, though stripped of its early purity and power, ceased to be operative toward the ultimate peace of the world. It was working away like leaven, cultivating the intellect, developing the instincts of freedom, preparing the ground for the building of modern independent, self-governing nations. Between Christians themselves, particularly those in private life, much of the early peace spirit and practice remained. The New Testament with its teaching of love and peace continued the same. They heard it read and expounded. The Saviour's life and example were often before them. Those who entered into official positions carried something of the Christian spirit with them. The *pax Romana* of the empire was softened and considerably humanized through the influence of the popes and bishops. They served as arbitrators in disputes between subject kings and feudal lords. They even dictated peace to emperors themselves. Though they did this often in the interest of their own dominion, substituting a *pax ecclesiastica* for the Roman imperial peace, nevertheless something of the real Christian spirit accompanied their work. During the interminable strifes of feudalism and the private wars of the Middle Ages, the bishops and church councils were about the only peace power which remained to check in any way the everlasting work of the sword. They proclaimed the " Peace of God," rendering sacred from bloodshed certain days and places. They hurled their anathemas at those wild barons who persisted in the practice of private war and the wager of battle. They denounced the duel, as the Church has always done. It was chiefly through their influence that private war, the wager of battle and the cruel " ordeal " were finally abolished — the first great triumph in the direction of political peace. They offered their services as conciliators, and created peace associations and church courts of arbitration. The Christian Church in its worst days never lost entirely the great peace conceptions of the Master, and never failed to show in some measure his spirit of peace.

During these dark times the instincts of pure humanity were at work also. No one retaining any remnants of human feeling could remain untouched by the cruel and never-ending carnage and massacre which characterized the first hundred years of the Reformation period, the sixteenth century. The very darkness of the period created the demand for light. The appalling contrast between the religion professed and the inhuman things daily done, between the demand of the human heart and the heartless deeds of the human hand, between the fraternal workings of trade and commerce, then first entering upon their grand modern development, and the unending disturbances and waste of wars, combined to bring about during the next century one of the greatest reactions known to history, the full force of which we have only in recent years begun to comprehend.

FOUR GREAT PEACE EVENTS OF THE SEVENTEENTH CENTURY

The seventeenth century brought to the world the first unfolding of the idea of international peace in a large and comprehensive way. Unlike the Christian movement of the first and second centuries, this evolution of the seventeenth century was not only religious and social, but also juridical and political. Four events of the seventeenth century, occurring in four different countries, the outcome of the thinking and work of four eminent men, have been the talk of much of the civilized world ever since, and may be considered the four cornerstones of the structure of modern peace work. They were all the outcome in different ways of the ripening of the time toward a larger feeling of brotherhood between peoples and nations, and a better social order. The first of them was the Great Design of Henry IV. of France, in the early years of the century, for the federation and peace of Christian Europe. The greatest in the line of French kings, Henry seems to have combined in his person the extraordinary contradictions of his time. A Protestant and a Catholic, rich and powerful, yet simple in manners and devoted to the interests of the common people, a warrior and a genuine friend of the peaceful arts of life, a Frenchman to the core, he was nevertheless the first interpreter to his country of the larger ideal of international life and coöperation then struggling to the birth. His Great Design was favorably received at more than one court in Europe. His death by assassination at the hands of Ravaillac cut the whole scheme short. The Design, though having a noble purpose, was full of contradictions. If he had lived to make the attempt seriously to carry it out, it is almost certain that the means by which he proposed to execute it — a great international army and the crushing of the House of Hapsburg — would have made the Design a worse wreck than that of the Holy Alliance two hundred years later. If we leave the means of execution out of sight, Henry's conception of Europe federated and in peace, about which his soul was said to have been deeply exercised, was a great one, and the vision has haunted the civilized world ever since. It has been immensely fruitful in holding thought and aspiration to the idea of closer union and more friendly coöperation among the nations — in other words, the federation of the world, the largest social conception of our time.

In 1625, fifteen years after the death of Henry IV., Hugo Grotius, whose patron the French king had been, published his famous book, " On the Rights of War and of Peace." This was the second of the four events. All his immense learning and his acquaintance with European affairs, gained through exile and diplomatic service, Grotius threw into an effort to lessen the cruelties and sufferings inflicted by war. He denounced in unmeasured terms the facility with which professedly Christian princes went to war, declaring their conduct to be a disgrace even to barbarians. He pleaded in a noble Christian spirit for the use of arbitration. His book immediately had an immense effect in Europe. It was as if the suffering spirit of the entire continent had dictated his words. The work set men to thinking seriously on the nature of war, on the duty of mitigating its horrors, and of trying to prevent its recurrence. Gustavus Adolphus, during his campaigns, is said to have slept with a copy of it under his head. Grotius's work was the foundation of international law, which has developed greatly since his time, and has gradually been carrying the ideas of justice, respect and mutual service into international affairs.

The third of the seventeenth century events to which I allude was the peace work of George Fox. Fox was born the year before Grotius published his book, and began his ministry twenty-three years later. The English peacemaker went much farther than the great Dutchman. He revived the early Christian position, feebly uttered before his time by the Mennonites and Moravians, that the spirit and teaching of Jesus leave no place whatever for war and the spirit out of which it springs. He incorporated this teaching as a fundamental in the doctrinal constitution of the Society of Friends. He uttered this principle with such marvellous energy, moral thoroughness, constancy and suffering endurance, that the whole English-speaking world was compelled to listen. No small part of Europe also heard his voice. Nor has the utterance ever been forgotten. Its maintenance in an organized way by the Friends has kept the high ideal of absolute and universal peace constantly before the eye of civilization as a guiding light. Great as was the work of Henry IV. in starting Europe to thinking on the subject of world-federation, or of Grotius in laying the foundations of international law, greater still was that of George Fox, because he not only declared his prin-

ciple, but gave it in trust for the future to a living
organism of men. His work has been in creative
power what that of Grotius would have been if he
had left a society of say a hundred thousand international lawyers possessed of more or less of his own
faith and enthusiasm.

The fourth of the seventeenth century events
alluded to was William Penn's Holy Experiment in
government on peace principles, inaugurated on this
side of the Atlantic in 1682. With this must be
coupled his Plan for the Peace of Europe, published
eleven years later in England, a scheme free from
the destructive contradictions of the Great Design
of Henry IV. Penn's experiment in practical peace
politics, the first of its kind in history, lasting more
than half a century, has become almost an inherent
part of the moral consciousness of the modern political world, and it is becoming every year more effective in creating a belief that war is always honor-
ably avoidable if men sincerely wish it to be avoided.

The works of these four men in the seventeenth
century, unlike as they were, were not isolated and
dissociated events. They all sprang, on their earthly
side, from the same root. They were the expression
of the growing sense of brotherhood, as yet scarcely
conscious of itself, which Christianity had been
silently creating, and of the developing consciousness
of the inhumanity of war, felt even while men

fought, gloried in combat, and lost their heads in the delirium of victory. They were heaven-begotten efforts, certainly, but they had their place in the providential historic development of the Christian world. Their immediate effects on the world as a whole were not large, but one has only to study them in the light of subsequent history to see what powerful seed-forces they were.

WORK OF THE EIGHTEENTH CENTURY

The movement of thought and purpose which these men of the seventeenth century interpreted with such insight and courage went steadily on into the eighteenth century. It found a number of distinguished representatives in different fields. The work of Grotius in international law was carried forward by Pufendorf, Vattel and others. The schemes of William Penn and Henry IV. were reproduced in France by the Abbé de St. Pierre (1713) and Rousseau, and later in England by Bentham. Adam Smith and Turgot, toward the close of the century, drew from economics powerful arguments for international intercourse and friendship. Poetry also, in this fruitful era, came forward to support the growing demand for peace, and Lessing and Herder uttered the new thought in verse. Even before the seventeenth century had closed, philosophy, through Locke, Leibnitz and

Montesquieu, had made its protest of reason against war. The last years of the eighteenth century gave us Kant's great tractate on " Perpetual Peace," in which was uttered for the first time the idea of a federation of the world in an international state built upon republican principles; and Kant's thought was vigorously sustained and developed by his followers, Fichte and Schelling.

For the most part the peace work of the eighteenth century was still theoretical and ideal. There was little attempt at the practical. The time had hardly come for it in any general way. Opinion was still too feeble and unintegrated. The Friends as a body continued their peace protest, but in a very traditional way, and many of them failed in the hour of testing. The colony of Pennsylvania abandoned the standard of Penn and fell away into the general condition of society round about. In the unfolding of ideas, theories and projects of peace the century was very prolific, but not until near its close did the movement veer much toward the practical. There were here and there some unimportant arbitrations, but they had little juridic character and passed almost unnoticed. They were mere temporary expedients of a personal rather than of a social character. The contentions and destructive conflicts of peoples and nations went on almost unrelieved. Diplomacy itself, which is essentially an

instrument of peace and originated as such, was
swept away and turned into an instrument of pro-
moting war and conquest. The eighteenth century,
in spite of St. Pierre, Bentham and Kant, and the
growing undercurrent of thought and aspiration
represented by them, closed with Napoleon over-
shadowing Europe and war still on the throne.

MOVEMENTS FOR LIBERTY AND FOR PEACE PROCEED TOGETHER

It is a noteworthy historic fact, deserving **mention**
in connection with the opening of the nineteenth
century, that the movement for the abolition of war
and that for human liberty went hand in hand.
Wherever the sense of liberty, civil or religious,
became well developed, respect for the rights of
other peoples appeared, and with it the feeling that
war ought to cease and peace prevail. The two are
really parts of the same movement, for slavery and
war spring out of the same spirit. The demand for
peace is a demand for justice, equal rights and universal liberty. William Penn was as consecrated to
liberty as to peace. He understood that without the
former the latter is impossible. The author of " Perpetual Peace " was so passionately devoted to liberty
that when he heard that a copy of the " Declaration
of the Rights of Man " had arrived from France,

he ran across the university campus at Königsberg,
a thing which he had never been known to do before. On the 14th of May, 1790, the French assembly, which met in the interests of liberty, solemnly decreed the abolition of war. The founders
of American liberty had a great fear of war and of
standing armies, and left no place for war except
as a last resort in the defense of liberty and rights.
Many of the leaders of the anti-slavery movement
— Whittier, Garrison, Jay, Ballou, Wright, May
and others — were absolute peace men. There is no
record of a real peace man who has not been an
uncompromising friend of liberty, though many
friends of liberty have failed to see that they ought
consistently to be uncompromising opponents of
war. The liberty movement of the last two centuries, resulting in independent republics in the New
World and constitutional governments in the Old,
has seen the peace propaganda spring up and de-
velop simultaneously and almost coterminously with
it. The nation which has taken the lead in the
development of liberty and the creation of institutions founded thereon has also led in the movement
for the abolition of war, on both its sentimental and
its practical side.

EVOLUTION OF THE MOVEMENT IN THE
NINETEENTH CENTURY

The nineteenth century saw a remarkable evolution of the movement for peace along many lines. The movement not only became much more extended, but it also became thoroughly organized and strongly practical. It did not, however, lose any of its idealism. It deepened and widened on its sentimental side quite as much as on its practical side. For every peace idealist whose name comes to us from the two previous centuries, the nineteenth furnishes scores. Noah Worcester, William Ladd, Jonathan Dymond, William E. Channing, Charles Sumner, Adin Ballou, Thomas C. Upham, Elihu Burritt, William Jay, John Bright, Richard Cobden, Henry Richard, Hodgson Pratt, Victor Hugo, Charles Lemonnier, Frédéric Passy, Bertha von Suttner, David Dudley Field, E. T. Moneta, Fredrik Bajer, Sheldon Amos, Bluntschli, Leone Levi, Leo Tolstoy, John de Bloch, and Nicholas II., to mention no others, all were primarily peace idealists. Some of them were nothing else, and were none the less useful for that reason. But the strong idealism which characterized the century's peace efforts did not prevent them from being singularly practical. In recent years the labors of the friends of peace, both in their individual and their organized capacity as societies and congresses, have consisted largely in efforts to secure the adoption of pacific methods of settling disputes. Their appeals to public sentiment have always had this end in view.

The bare mention of the list of names just given — and it could be increased indefinitely — gives a vivid impression of the great expansion of peace thought and work as compared with former times. When the nineteenth century opened not a peace society existed. There was no thought of organization. There had been no coöperation of thinkers and workers, if it can be said that there were any workers. The Friends had not gone beyond their own borders to coöperate with others. But after 1815 organization was effected and developed to such an extent that there are to-day peace associations and unions to the number of more than four hundred, in no less than fifteen countries, numbering many thousands of adherents, coming from all classes of society. Besides these, many other organizations — church clubs, women's clubs, the temperance union, business organizations, working men's unions — give peace a large place in their programs. Between these numerous friends of peace in different countries a close bond has been formed. Peace congresses and conferences are a part of the settled order of the day. The International Peace Bureau at Berne, in existence now for more than a dozen years, has made the union permanent. In Kant's day statesmen were so far from giving peace any place in their thought that he delicately apologized to them in his " Perpetual Peace " for venturing to suggest that his treatise might not do them any damage. To-day, only a little over a hundred years from his time, the largest peace organization in existence, the Interparliamentary Peace Union, with more than two thousand members, consists wholly of statesmen, who meet annually or biennially in European and American cities to promote the settlement of international differences by arbitration. One can easily imagine Kant running again across the university campus at knowledge of this remarkable organization.

At the beginning of the nineteenth century there had been no cases of international arbitration of any great importance. Since then the method has come into general use, more than two hundred important cases having been settled by this means. All the civilized nations have had recourse to arbitration, some of them many times. Difficulties of almost every sort have been adjusted in this way. The legislatures of nearly all the civilized nations have passed strong resolutions favoring the employment of arbitration in the adjustment of disputes. In industrial controversies the principle of arbitration has made no less signal progress. The labor organizations and the socialist movements, representing millions of both men and women, are placing themselves everywhere against war and standing armies as instruments of tyranny and economic oppression. International law as a means of preventing and mitigating war has also made great advance since the opening of the nineteenth century. It has given us the principle of neutrality, which prevents war from spreading and involving a whole group of nations, as was the case only a century ago. It has given us the Red Cross, which pitches its tents of mercy right in the midst of the blood-red field. It has carried the principles of right and justice a good way into the chaos of international affairs. It operates over a wide field of international relations in time of peace, cultivating acquaintance, friendship and restraint of passion. In time of war it prevents, in considerable measure, cruelties and sufferings forming no necessary part of fighting and campaigning, but which formerly attended every war.

THE PEACE IDEA IN LITERATURE

The peace idea has entered deeply into modern literature. You could count on the fingers of two hands all the valuable works on peace which appeared prior to the year 1800. Since then a body of special peace literature has grown up so extensive that it is doubtful if fifty duodecimo pages would hold the bare list of titles of books and pamphlets which have been published. This takes no account of the innumerable articles which have appeared in recent years in the magazines and newspapers, nor of the treatment of the subject in general literature by authors like Tennyson, Whittier, Longfellow and many others of equal or less note.

NATURAL FORCES AT WORK

At no previous time in history have the natural peace forces — association, trade, commerce, travel, and the like — operated so powerfully as within the last fifty years. Modern methods of intercommunication have put all parts of the complex modern world into incessant touch with each other. The daily rubbing, grinding and clashing of these parts occasionally result in a dreadful clash of war which horrifies us, but the general effect is exactly the opposite. Men are thereby brought into fuller knowledge of one another, are trained in self-restraint, are made more patient and forbearing, and are led to see and feel their interdependence and their power of mutual service. Thus is worked out in a practical way the feeling of universal kinship and brotherhood, to take the place of, or rather to enlarge, the narrow idea of family kinship which has controlled the world in the past. This practical enlargement of vision, of sympathy, of community of interests, is developing, or rather has already developed, among the masses of men a general fear and abhorrence of war which not even the most popular particular war long interferes with. The war between Japan and Russia, which has just come to an end, has been deeply deplored throughout the entire civilized world, and its close has been everywhere hailed with inexpressible delight. Just here in this abhorrence of war and love of settled order lies the largest practical gain which the cause of peace has made.

THE HAGUE CONFERENCE AND WHAT HAS FOLLOWED IT

The Hague Conference, held in 1899, is, with its results, so far the largest practical expression of this long historic development of the peace idea. Its full significance is yet but imperfectly understood. This great Conference, which was directed by men of the highest attainment in diplomatic affairs, sat for ten weeks, and resulted in the drafting of a scheme for a permanent international court of arbitration. This Convention was ratified by twenty-two of the governments represented, and is now in full force.

The setting up of this Court and the successful inauguration of its work mark the close of a wonderful century in the development of the movement for international peace. It likewise marks the opening of a new page in the history which, unless all signs fail, is sure to be more wonderful than the last. Quickly following the inauguration of the International Court of Arbitration have come the numerous treaties of obligatory arbitration concluded among the nations of Europe and of South America. But the movement has already gone beyond these limited treaties, and the peace societies, the peace congresses, the Interparliamentary Union, business organizations, etc., are demanding the conclusion of a general arbitration treaty among all the civilized nations which shall bring the Hague Court into regular and if possible universal use in the adjustment of controversies, and thus establish finally the reign of law in international affairs. Further than this, the demand has arisen, and already taken a commanding place in the peace propaganda, for the creation of a regular parliament or congress of the nations for the orderly treatment of international problems. A second conference at The Hague has already been called, and its meeting is awaited with the greatest public interest, for it is expected that it will go much beyond the work of the first Hague Conference in the permanent organization of the peace of the world.

Reasoning purely from the history already made, we may easily in imagination construct, on the foundations now well laid, the temple of international peace which another hundred years will see largely completed. All the forces which have hitherto been working are mightier to-day than ever before. What made the Hague Conference will make others like it, probably in regular succession. What brought the Permanent Court of Arbitration into existence will cause the ultimate reference to it of all international controversies. What has made the remarkable movement in South America, led by Chile and the Argentine Republic, will work on until it has mastered the Continent. What created the present crude, but none the less real, world-society will enlarge and perfect it, until not a foot of the earth's surface and not a man of its inhabitants remain unsocialized and unfederated with the rest. The international competitive system, which has grown largely out of selfishness, ambition and greed, is nearing its end. The great armaments springing therefrom, which are crushing the world with their burdensomeness and threatening to wreck civilization, have grown so intolerable that they cannot long survive. Christianity, commerce, industry, labor, education, social culture, the common weal, in their recent development, are all against war. However discouraging present appearances may seem, its days are nearly numbered. It will die hard, but die it must. History has already written its death-warrant on the wall, and whatever God has written in history is written.

THE CHRISTIAN CHURCH AND PEACE

I ought not to close this paper before a religious gathering like this without saying one thing more. Jesus Christ has been behind the peace movement in all its phases. There was no such movement until he came. He set forth the great principle of the divine kinship of men which inspired it. He exemplified this in an example which has ever since been like a sun in the social heavens. He kept the spirit and hope of peace alive through all the dark centuries. It was he who revived them in the seventeenth century, and strengthened and developed them during the eighteenth. Through his inspiration Christian men and ministers of the gospel gave us the organized peace movement of our time. During no inconsiderable periods of the past century disciples of his furnished its chief and practically only support. Until quite recently most of the distinguished advocates of peace were professedly Christian men and women. The record which the peace movement has made is fundamentally due to them. Profoundly grateful as we must be to the distinguished men and women beyond the pale of the Christian profession who in recent years have been among the chiefest apostles of the cause, yet fidelity to historic fact demands the recognition of the primacy of Christianity in the founding and developing of the work of peace.

I am sorry to have to say that, while through individual men Christianity has led the whole historic peace movement, the Church as a whole has been criminally unfaithful, and does not yet show any strong tendency to return to the original Christian position, or any high position, on the subject of peace. An increasing number of its ministers and members are, however, returning to that position. Tolstoy, whom the Orthodox Greek Church has excommunicated for his arraignment of her barren formality and her support of war, is not the only man of primitive Christian thought on the subject. It would be easy to find a good two hundred thousand of like principles in different parts of the earth. In the mission field a number of the great pioneers — Livingstone, Titus Coan, J. Hudson Taylor — renounced all dependence on carnal weapons even for self-defence. Many of their less known followers and co-workers share and practise their views.

The evolution of the peace movement ought to proceed much more rapidly within the Church than without. Is it doing so? One feels the sting of pain when one sees the Church and its ministry lashed by outsiders — splendid men and women of peace — because so many professed Christians and so many preachers of the gospel uphold the system of war, or particular wars, which these outsiders see cannot live an hour in the light of the New Testament. In our endeavors to promote the development of the peace cause, we must begin our judgment at the house of God. We must insist, with every artifice of appeal, that those who call themselves by Christ's name shall be true to Christ's spirit. We must keep in the forefront of all our work the great principle of human brotherhood, without which Christianity is not Christianity, but at best only a refined religion of self-righteousness. This principle of brotherhood is the great instrument with which we must work. It is only in its enlargement and ever wider practical application that the idea of social and international peace came into existence. It is the central pillar on which the new International Court of Arbitration must rest for its permanence and efficiency. There cannot be further development unless this principle is given a larger place. It is far from triumphant to-day, even in Christian society. There is disloyalty to it in a thousand ways of which men are scarcely conscious. There is retrogression from it in certain high places. If history shows anything plainly, it shows that sense of kinship and brotherhood is the root from which all peace springs. This lesson of history must be taken more seriously to heart, and must be given the widest world-application by all those who seek to bring in the era of world-peace.

While God by the ordinary course of his providences is working out the spirit of fraternity and peace by the great social and economic forces operating naturally in society, it is the Christian's high privilege to hasten the movement by following his Master in the life of self-sacrificing and universal love, which cannot possibly from self-interest kill human beings, but which gives life freely and ungrudgingly to save men of all classes and conditions. So far as lies in our power, we must not allow to be set up or kept up anywhere within the Church the walls between classes, races and nationalities which the Master levelled to the ground. We must declare our faith in the brotherhood of mankind and the sisterhood of nations in the face of the spurious patriotism which in its pride of country and race rides roughshod over uncivilized races and weak peoples, and is always watching for an opening into which to drive its self-seeking power.

At the point of development which the peace movement has reached, this is the supreme service which the Christian Church, in all its membership, is divinely commissioned to perform. If the Church, which is now a commanding institution in the civilized world, is willing to lose its life in this way with the Master, it shall find it again at no distant day in a world at peace at the feet of the Prince of Peace.

WILLIAM PENN'S HOLY EXPERI-
MENT IN CIVIL GOVERNMENT [1]

T HE first knowledge that I ever had of the noble statue which now crowns your great municipal building came to me in a rather curious way. Years ago when the work of constructing the building was not more than half completed I chanced to be in the city. Walking one day up Market Street toward the Broad Street station, I enquired of a gentleman who was with me what the cost of the edifice was likely to be when completed. He gave me approximately the cost up to that time, and said that nobody could guess what the expense of the future work would be. He then added, with a significant smile, that it was proposed to cover up the stock-jobbery connected with its erection by placing a statue of William Penn in his broadbrim on the top of it.

This was my introduction to the statue in connection with the placing of which I have been invited to say a few words about William Penn's

---

[1] Delivered at a public commemorative service in Association Hall, Philadelphia, December 14, 1894, at the time of the placing of the statue of William Penn on the City Hall.

experiment in Christian statesmanship. I am sure, after the little avalanche of municipal righteousness which has recently descended upon several of our cities, that you will agree with me when I say that the lifting of this statue of the great Quaker to the summit of your city hall means something more than the mere covering up of some stock-jobbery, more or less, which may have been connected with its erection. May we not take it as a prophecy of the entire banishment from your city life of all municipal crookedness and pollution, and of the enthronement in our common country, for you and for us all, of that principle of brother-love — divine, all comprehensive, practical — out of which all Penn's work grew. This principle he has enshrined in the name which every citizen of this great city speaks and hears spoken every day of his life. Philadelphia, brother-love! That is the message of the silent lips of the founder to the great Commonwealth to-day. That is the thing which human society, after its long sorrowful centuries of bitter hate and endless bloodshed, is slowly learning to recognize as " the greatest thing in the world "; the real secret of all that is worthy and enduring in its progress.

The story of William Penn, in its marvellous uniqueness and its unmistakable participation in the supernatural, has always read to me much like a myth out of the olden time. Not that there is anything shadowy or unreal about it, for in the entire annals of the race no bit of history is more authentic and clear. So many of the original documents are preserved in the archives of your own Historical Society and elsewhere that the man stands before us worshipping, loving, preaching, writing, creating charters, making treaties, governing, settling difficulties, allaying disorders, defending himself against injustice and wrong, giving away his life and fortune, and breaking down under abuse and ingratitude, in as lifelike a way as if he were still the governor of the Commonwealth which he founded on this spot two hundred twelve years ago. Not only is his history incomparably clear, but it is also clearly unlike any other piece of human history. In its grasp of the principles of liberty, equality and brotherhood, and of the secret of their successful establishment among men, and particularly in its heroic application of these principles and of this secret in the constitution and government of a Commonwealth, it stands apart an absolutely unique chapter in the history of men and of States. It was a " holy experiment " because it was founded in love, built up on the principles which love dictates and carried forward in the faith which is inspired and sustained by love.

For the sake of clearness in the historic picture, let us consider, in order, the purpose of the experiment, the conditions under which it was tried, the success which attended it, and the influence which it has exerted.

Briefly stated, William Penn's purpose in buying of the king lands here in America and in preparing a charter for the government of the colony which he was proposing to plant was that he might establish a Christian State, based from the start on Christian principle, created and directed in the spirit of Christian love, a State in which the governing and the governed might realize together the blessings of the brotherhood taught by Jesus Christ. He reasoned that if Christianity is true, if the principles of Christ's mountain instruction are obligatory for the individual, they must be no less so for the State. He had verified these principles in his own experience; he would therefore seize the opportunity which the providence of God had given him, to test their practicability, of which he had not the slightest doubt, in the wider circle of the State.

In order to understand fully the real nature of his purpose, we must go to its root and remember that it was founded in the Christian doctrine of love. He did not lead forth a colony that he and they might simply escape the tyrannies of the old world and struggle together for freedom, for independence, and self-government in the new. He led it forth that he might give it the love which Christ had created in his own soul, and as the head of a State exemplify those forms of benevolence and practical righteousness which spring from this great life-root. The purpose had in it freedom, independence, equality of privilege and self-government of the highest order, but these were to be the fruit of the tree rather than the tree itself. Everywhere love, thinking and planning and living for others, was to be the creating and controlling motive, and whatever could not be done in love was not to be done at all. Whoever misses this point of view can never understand the nature of the " holy experiment " nor comprehend the mutual relation of its different parts. Many historians have lauded William Penn's services to the cause of civil and religious liberty, but have failed to grasp this secret of the experiment, and hence have considered his abandonment of the sword and his almost complete dependence on the moral power of truth and of Christian kindness and self-giving as a well-meant but unfortunate bit of religious sentimentalism and as the fatal weakness of the whole undertaking. On the contrary, I venture to say that this pacific policy was not only an essential part of the scheme but its distinguishing feature and glory. Without it the experiment would have been vitiated and would have differed in no essential respect from other experiments in free government which were being made on these shores. In fact, it would have been impossible. There would have been no one to make it. So that whatever praise is due to the experiment is due to it because it was a peace-experiment dictated by the love which works no ill to one's neighbor. Lands had been bought of the natives in several other parts of the colonies. Carver had made a treaty with Massasoit at Plymouth, which had been faithfully kept for fifty years, but it was a defensive war alliance, the native warriors in their accoutrements being present on the one side and Miles Standish with his standing army of six men in line on the other. Roger Williams and Lord Baltimore had introduced religious toleration into the colonies of Rhode Island and Maryland, as had Locke and Shaftesbury in the Carolinas. It is true that Penn went further in the principles of pure democracy than was the case in the other colonies, but he did this for the same reason that led him to banish the sword, and there were not a few occasions in the early history of the colony when the absence of the sword proved to be the greatest safe-guard of the liberties of the infant democracy. No! the peace plank in his platform of principles was cut from the same tree as all the rest. The heart that loved his fellowmen so fully that it was impossible for him even to wear the sword against them was the only heart in England at that time that knew the outmost meaning of human rights, human liberties and human equalities. A Commonwealth of love, justice, liberty, equal rights and peace — that was what this Christian statesman proposed to found.

What were the conditions under which this experiment in Christian statesmanship had to be made? In order to understand the difficulty and to appreciate the heroism of the task and to measure rightly the success of the undertaking, it must be remembered that the characteristics of the time, on both sides of the Atlantic, were, both in principle and in practice, totally contrary to what William Penn proposed to do. It was an age of war and selfishness and cruelty; an age of suspicion and treason and judicial murder; an age of greed and envy and betrayal; of persecution and imprisonment and torture, when a man's life was scarcely worth the hat which he wore on his head. Intolerance was the very soul of that epoch. Cromwell and his Ironsides were gone, after having swept all England with the sword, in the name of liberty. The polluted and frivolous and persecuting Charles II. was still on the throne when Penn's experiment began in 1682. Then came James II., smooth of tongue but cruel of heart, whose reign, in spite of the relief which he gave to the Friends, was an intolerable civil and religious despotism, during which the diabolical Chief Justice Jeffreys went round his Bloody Circuit and returned from it to receive the Great Seal and to boast that he had hanged more persons for high treason than all the judges of England since William the Conqueror. The struggle for liberty and toleration which was still in its infancy, which was rendered desperate by the atrocious cruelties committed by James's minions and which finally brought on the revolution which placed William III. on the throne, everywhere armed itself with the sword and knew little of any other means of attaining its end.

William Penn was by birth a son of this time. Its instincts were in his blood. He was born and reared a soldier. His ancestry for two generations had been men of war. But for the miracle of grace which converted him to pure New Testament Christianity and subdued the fighting nature within him, he would most probably have become the admiral of an English fleet or the commander of an army and have stained his hands with blood in defence of the liberty and toleration of that particular party into which the accident of birth had cast him. He had, therefore, as the divinely appointed prophet and leader of a new age to break not only with his time but also with his own flesh and blood. The difficulties of his undertaking were heightened by the fact that outside of his own religious connection he had few sympathizers. There was in all England

scarcely any man except Algernon Sidney who entered intelligently into his broad conception of civil
liberty, and Sidney was a man of war spirit. If Penn,
then, was driven by the religious and political intolerance and narrowness of his time and by the
impulses of a great freedom and of a great love
within him to seek a home for liberty in the new
world, what sympathy and support could he expect
from his mother country where intolerance reigned
and where the clash of arms was always heard, if,
that is, he should attempt to set up and maintain his
free commonwealth without an appeal to the sword?
It is scarcely to be wondered at that England laughed
merrily at the supposed stupidity of her Quaker son.
King Charles, if the traditional interview between
him and Penn is to be trusted, doubtless expressed
the general feeling of astonishment at Penn's rash-
ness, when he said, " I have no idea of any security
against those cannibals but in a regiment of good
soldiers with their muskets and bayonets." Penn
must have known, then, not only that this distrust
of his method would follow him, but also that the
militarism of western Europe would sooner or later
throw its baleful influence across the Atlantic to the
banks of the Delaware around and into the very
colony which he was planting.

In fact, the greedy, intolerant, narrow and fighting spirit of the old world was already in the new,

so that the conditions existing in 1682 on this side
of the Atlantic were not much more encouraging
for the experiment than those on the other. Religious intolerance from which the Pilgrims had fled
and which Penn wished to make forever impossible
in his colony had already appeared and was destined
to run a course of obstinate cruelty, " not unworthy
the best days of the Star Chamber and the Court of
Inquisition." To what extent religious persecution
had gone in the Virginia colonies and especially in
New England every true American would be only
too glad to forget, and the rope by which some of
his own fellow religionists had been hanged had
scarcely been taken down when Penn began to plan
for his experiment. Political tyranny was likewise
trying to throttle the nascent liberties of the colonies,
and that conflict was already under way which
finally resulted in the revocation of most of the colonial charters and in the placing of most of the new
commonwealths directly under the control of the
Crown. There was a third and even greater danger
to the undertaking as the sequel proved. That contest for the mastery of North America which
reached its culmination in the war between France
and England in 1755–59 was already beginning to
throw its bloody shadow over the country. It was
to the pressure of this contest that Pennsylvania
finally yielded and abandoned the peace policy.

Then, again, the Indians had been rendered suspicious and vindictive in nearly all parts of the colonies by the treatment which they had met with at the hands of the whites. The fact that they were a race of savages, wholly unacquainted with the elementary principles of Christianity, following as the law of their life their animal instincts, engaged in almost incessant inter-tribal wars and brutalized into blood-thirsty scalpers, would in itself have made the experiment seem difficult enough to an ordinary man. But colonization had been going on for sixty years, and during all this period the settlers had not only met the Indians on the plane of force but had often wrested their lands from them by violence or trickery and had treated them as if they possessed no rights to the soil, or even no rights at all.

From the days of Carver and Miles Standish on, the whites in New England had met the Red Men on the plane of force.[1] The tension between the two

---

[1] It is not intended by what is said here that the Pilgrims were unfriendly to the Indians. The contrary is true. But they did proceed, in their relations with them, on the basis of force. They established a militia at the outset, and in less than three years from their arrival Miles Standish and his men went in pursuit of some Indians who had manifested hostile intentions, provoked by some of the colonists who were not Pilgrims, and killed a number of them. What is meant is that the presence of soldiers and implements of war and the intention to use them in defending and avenging themselves brought the settlers

races became greater and greater until in 1675, only seven years before Penn arrived, King Philip's war had broken out and for a whole year massacre, burning and desolation reigned everywhere. The wild war whoop was heard by probably every family in Massachusetts, New Hampshire, Rhode Island and Connecticut, and six hundred white men, the pick and pride of the country, fell in battle. The Red Men were swept out of New England, but only to spread disaffection and the spirit of revenge to the West and South. The disaffection of the natives in the other parts of the colonies was equally great, and from the same causes. In Virginia the first settlers had built a fort and placed sentinels on guard. One has only to read the romantic but inhuman and vengeful life of Captain John Smith to understand why there was always trouble with the Indians on the borders of Maryland and Virginia and three general Indian wars and massacres before these colonies were fifty years old. In the settlements of New York and vicinity the same line of policy had been followed in the treatment of the Indians with the same sad and desolating results. In the Carolinas the treatment of the natives was

---

inevitably into deadly conflict with the natives. Their varied manifestations of kindness were not powerful enough to prevent the mischievous effects of the gun and soldier policy which they pursued.

even more degrading, and they were fast disappearing through the influence of drink and the fraudulent and forcible occupation of their hunting grounds, while those who still remained were jealous and revengeful.

At the time when Penn came, therefore, he found, not the original natives of the forests warlike and fierce but at the same time open-minded and trustful, but a race filled with distrust and hatred of the whites and cherishing a sullen, cunning, unrelenting spirit of vengeance. It is not strange that King Charles thought they might have Penn in their war-kettle in two hours after his arrival. Penn himself did not treat as a trivial thing the possible dangers awaiting him and his colonists from a race accustomed to the tomahawk, the scalping knife and the war-kettle, and whose dislike for the whites was so deep-seated and apparently implacable.

What hope, then, was there that the new colony in which civil and religious liberty and equality were carried to the extreme of universal suffrage and universal toleration, with not a soldier to defend its rights, could live a year under such conditions as have just been shown to exist on both sides of the Atlantic? From the ordinary human standpoint, absolutely none. But Penn's was neither the ordinary nor the human standpoint, as generally conceived. But he had already tried the strength of his new faith against English kings and English mobs, against perverted judges and soulless officers, in English prisons and the Tower, and whatever might be the outcome of this larger effort to help his fellow-men he would brave every difficulty and do his duty.

Of the success of the experiment it is easy and at the same time somewhat difficult to speak, so different are the standards by which men judge of success. Fortunately, in the case before us, success followed so many different lines that no one has ever dared to say that the experiment was a failure.

Not the least remarkable of its successes was the fact that Penn himself was true to his own ideal of Christian statesmanship till the end of his life — thirty-six years after he first came to the new world. After the most critical sifting of his history, through which the strictures of Macaulay and Bishop Burnet and Dr. Franklin have been shown to be utterly unfair and ungracious, not a deed, not a line, scarcely a word of his can be found with which to reproach him for faltering, much less for worldliness or duplicity. His unselfish devotion to the good of mankind grew greater to the last. He loved his Commonwealth, and gave himself for it. He might have built up a colossal fortune through his proprietary rights, the granting of monopolies and restrictions on trade. But he resisted all the seductions of wealth, that others might be free and happy and prosperous. He was true to his promise that the colony should be free and self-governing. His powers as governor he allowed to be gradually restricted, that neither he nor any of his successors might ever be able to work mischief. The representatives sent up by the universal suffrage of the people made the laws, and when the charter was found to be inadequate to the growing needs of the community, he freely gave them a new or modified one. It is a waste of time to stop to say that he was loyal to the principle of religious toleration. No man of any nation or of any religious creed was allowed to be persecuted for his faith or for his lack of one. He sat as judge himself in the only case of witchcraft ever tried in Pennsylvania, and the superstition died under his eye. He adopted a humane, reformatory system of prison management, which England did not reach for more than a hundred years afterwards. He abolished capital punishment for all crimes except murder and treason, and hanging even for these was practically unknown in the colony. He established a system of universal intellectual and industrial education. He kept his purpose that no soldier or emblem of war should, by his authority, be seen in the Commonwealth. Even his police, when there were any, he did not arm. He set up courts of law in the counties, but to prevent

8246

suits he also established in each of them boards of arbitration. When misunderstandings and contentions arose in the Assembly, or in different parts of the Commonwealth, he allayed them by kindness, considerateness and patience. His letters from England were full of the same spirit, and were nearly as efficacious as his presence in person. In his last appeal from England, so great was the force of his letter to the colonists that not a single member of the old Assembly was returned at the new election. He bought the Indians' lands, made his famous treaty with them, and, without exception, treated them as brothers and friends, and his single power over them was literally greater than that of all the soldiers who ever crossed the Atlantic. It is certainly something akin to the highest kind of success, that for thirty-six years, as Proprietary, Governor and Statesman, the ideal of Christian leadership which he had set for himself he maintained without spot or wrinkle, in the face of so much that was harassing and discouraging.

In the second place, he succeeded in defending the liberties of his colony against the encroachments of English greed and tyranny, which more than once threatened to engulf them. He came to America to make it his permanent home, but he spent here only four out of his thirty-six remaining years. Going back after two years to defend the cause of religious toleration, he found himself compelled to defend himself and the possession of his charter against the machinations of his powerful enemies at the English Court. He stood in the breach alone, and broke the force of all the shafts of misrepresentation that were hurled at him, by the simple power of his transparent, straightforward Christian manhood. His rights in the colony as Governor, which were for a short time taken from him, were speedily restored. A second time the storm broke forth in a new way. The rapid growth of the colonies and their development in free government awakened the envy and the fear of England, and a movement was set on foot to take up all the proprietary rights, and to place the colonies under the direct control of the Crown and a military government. This, Penn could not think of allowing in the case of his colony, and hastening back to England he threw all the weight of his influence in Parliament and at the Court against the scheme. As years went on, and the Colonial Assembly began to treat him with the basest ingratitude, and his failing fortunes made it necessary for him to obtain money from some source he finally became willing to sell his proprietary rights to the Crown, but on the express condition that his Frame of Government should be maintained, and the liberties and independence of the colony in no wise interfered with.

This condition the Crown refused to accept, and the sale was never consummated. Others of the American commonwealths were finally seized by the Crown, but Pennsylvania, through Penn's influence at court (which lasted long after his death), remained under the form of government which he had given it until the Revolution severed forever its connection with the mother country. The constitution which grew up under his hand is, in its most essential features, the constitution of your great State to-day, and more, perhaps, than any other political document lies at the basis of the Constitution of the United States.

The people, also, whom Penn drew to his territory were among the most liberty-loving of all Europe. No sooner was his Frame of Government published, and his broad, humane spirit known, than multitudes from England, Wales, Scotland, Ireland, Holland, Germany, Sweden and elsewhere began to flock to the banks of the Delaware. The growth of the colony was extraordinary, and its chief characteristics were its high moral character, its good order, and its intense love of freedom. The people, because of their diverse origin and their early habits and customs, were often turbulent and sometimes selfish and hard to manage, but they almost without exception were at heart deeply devoted to the cause of civil and religious liberty, and it is no exaggeration to say that, on the whole, no other colony contributed so much to the development and final establishment of liberty and independence in this great country as that which was moulded by the spirit and the political measures of William Penn. It was fitting, then, that the Declaration of Independence and the building and signing of our national Constitution should have taken place on the very spot consecrated by him to the freedom and highest moral development of mankind.

Penn's Indian policy, which was only the more conspicuous part of his general peace policy, was marked by the greatest of all his successes. The treaty of Shackamaxon, called " the fairest page in American history," " the only treaty never sworn to, and never broken," differed from the treaty made by Carver, and from all other treaties with which the attempt has been made to compare it, not only in being altogether a peace treaty, but in being, in reality, not a treaty with one sachem or tribe only, but with the whole Indian race at that time and for all time. The Indians were disarmed even before the treaty was made. When Penn told them that it was not the custom of himself and of his followers to use weapons of war against their fellow-men, and that therefore they had come to the council un-armed, the Chief Taminent placed on his head a chaplet, into which was twisted a little horn, and at this signal all the Indian warriors laid down their weapons. It is a commonplace of our history that this treaty was not violated by the Indians until it was violated by the white men of the colony. For more than thirty years after Penn's death, so strongly did the Indians feel that all Pennsylvania must be in character like the founder, that they did not retaliate when wronged until trespass was heaped upon trespass, and no open rupture came until the peace party was outvoted in the General Assembly, and the colony armed herself for war. When she took the sword, the sword devoured her. The fury of war, with its horrible Indian massacres, swept over her once peaceful soil, and her history lost its fine uniqueness and became stained on many pages with blood.

With the real followers of Penn, the great treaty never was broken by the Indians, because they themselves never broke it. No Quaker blood was shed in Pennsylvania during the years of cruel war which followed the arming of the colony. Francis Parkman has labored hard in his brilliant pages to show that this oft-made statement is not true. But the Boston historian, whose nature was essentially bellicose, and who came dangerously near to accepting the theory that " there is no good Indian but a dead Indian," seems not to have been able to distinguish between a true and a nominal Quaker. It is true that a few persons who abandoned their principles by arming themselves and taking sides with the war party, were slain, though they tried to protect themselves with the Quaker name; but they were no more Quakers than a black man is a white one.[1] The treaty was not only kept during those times, but it has been kept ever since, with the true followers of Penn. Quaker men and women have associated in all conceivable ways with the Red Men in all parts of the land during the "century of dishonor" in our relations with them since the signing of the Constitution. They have established homes in their midst, have founded and maintained schools among them, have taught them the arts of industry and instructed them in Christianity; they have acted as government agents and inspectors, and

---

[1] Even if it could be shown that a few genuine Friends were slain during these or other wars, this would not prove as against the large number of cases of the opposite kind that the policy of peace is valueless from the standpoint of safety. No intelligent advocate of the policy has ever claimed that it would, if consistently maintained, secure absolute immunity from death by violence in all cases. Right and Christian duty, not safety, are the chief reasons urged in its support. And yet the many remarkable cases of preservation of Friends during the wars in Pennsylvania in the 18th century, in Ireland during the latter part of the same century and in the South during our civil war prove that peace principles faithfully maintained have a very high, if not complete, protective value.

have gone boldly among them when they were on the war-path, and when the war-dance was on, but no tomahawk has ever been lifted against one who was known to be a " Broadhat." The stars still shine and the rivers still run down to the sea, and Indian and Quaker alike, though standing in important respects over against each other at the opposite poles of civilization, have been true to the pledges made under the old elm tree.

As to the Commonwealth, the peace experiment was successful for seventy years, though a considerable part of the colony always opposed it and clamored for arms. Seventy years of peace in the turbulent atmosphere of that time meant much more than it would mean now, and is as near a demonstration as anything short of actual trial could be that the same thing might be done again by any state or nation whose people were convinced that it ought to be done and who had the courage to try it. The policy of peace never failed in Pennsylvania; Pennsylvania simply abandoned it. If it had been faithfully persisted in, that is, if governors and councils and assemblies and a sufficient majority of the people had continued to be, in spirit and in deed, like Penn and his first helpers, I for one have the faith, or, if you please to call it so, the credulity, to believe that Pennsylvania would have preserved her rights and liberties inviolate, that the French and Indian war would have missed her territory, that no Indian massacre would ever have polluted her soil, that the revolutionary war might through her influence have been avoided, or, at least, that Pennsylvania herself would have come through to complete and final independence, in union with the other colonies, without having shed any man's blood or having lost a drop of her own.

It was inevitable, as we see it now, that this peace policy in the government of the colony should sooner or later be abandoned. There were not people enough, unfortunately, who believed in it, to keep it up. Of the numbers who poured in from all parts of Europe only a few had any real understanding of or sympathy with the principles out of which it grew. This class came gradually to prevail among the population and in the halls of legislation. Even Penn's immediate successors in the governorship and proprietorship but feebly maintained his strength of conviction, his energy and his wisdom, and those farther removed were restless to throw overboard his peace policy long before the legislative body untied their hands. No policy could live under such conditions, for policies are little more than breath or paper unless they have back of them men out of whose life they spring, or whose convictions make them essentially their own. But the failure of the policy to stand under the circumstances and its pre-

vious success for a period nearly two-thirds as long
as our entire national life are both proofs of its
superior excellence, and more particularly of the
unsurpassed greatness and glory of the man who
created it and almost alone maintained it against
the world so long.

Though the policy was finally abandoned, the
experiment with it has exercised and still continues
to exercise a great and growing educational influence in our national life. While turning over the
leaves of our history, the eyes of our school children
have never missed the pages written by William
Penn. Admiration for him, though often lying
away unexpressed, has been as genuine and not un-
frequently as great as that for the men who have
fought for our liberties on the field of battle. The
peace sentiment which has always been strong
among our people, which has inspired some of the
noblest utterances of men of the highest national
fame — Washington, Franklin, Grant, Sherman,
Sumner, Garrison, Whittier, Longfellow, Lowell
— and which is more and more shaping our foreign
policies and dictating the solution of our industrial
problems owes much to the vivid object lesson which
he gave. This lesson has been silently but irresistibly
shaping the ideal of the nation. Through its influence, standing there like a magnificent statue of
light, we have finally thrown overboard, I believe

forever, the detestable Indian policy whose cruel inhumanity might well rank us among the most sordidly selfish and tyrannical peoples of history, a policy equalled in wickedness only by our former treatment of the black man, the movement for whose freedom likewise began on this selfsame spot under the influence of Penn. The influence of his object lesson, coöperating with other forces of course, has brought us up to the point where we are now rapidly establishing boards of arbitration and conciliation just like those which he set up in the primeval forests. It has done much toward making us a nation without arms and armies. It is making us the mediator among the contending nations of the earth. It is an unequivocal protest, which will some day be heard and heeded, against the present effort to militarize the youth of our land, through the schools and the churches, and against the stealthily growing but un-American ambition of a certain portion of our people that the United States should become the war-mistress of the seas.

The " holy experiment " will never again be made under anything like the conditions which existed at the close of the seventeenth century. It belonged to its own time, and in the same form will never be repeated. It was, as it was doubtless God's purpose that it should be, not only a protest against the wickedness of the time but a divine indication of what government is everywhere to be when the Christ-spirit shall have subdued the world. It is not likely that a State will ever be set up again, as Pennsylvania was, without swords and spears to be beaten ultimately into instruments of industry, but civilization is plodding slowly, surely upward along the lines marked out by him whose work we commemorate to-night, and all nations will one day drop their armor, disband their armies, call home their sea-dogs and rule thereafter by love and moral force alone. At that day William Penn, who dared both as individual and as statesman and ruler to keep, not simply the whole moral law, but the whole Christian law of life, will be considered, not the hero of your Commonwealth alone, but chief among the chief heroes of our national history and of all history, the first and greatest statesman-prophet and exemplar of the coming age of love and peace.

THE GOLDEN RULE IN
INTERNATIONAL AFFAIRS[1]

THE Golden Rule has been on the lips of the Christian world for nearly nineteen hundred years. It ought long ago to have become the controlling principle in all civilised social affairs, private, national and international. It contains in a condensed form the whole applied moral philosophy of life. But, strange to say, even its meaning has never been understood, except by a few people, and those mostly among the obscure. The admiration and praise of it uttered from pulpits and platforms, found in books, and sometimes heard in conversation, have been largely of a poetic, sentimental and æsthetic character, like that bestowed upon a precious stone, an exquisite statue, or a rare specimen in a showcase. " All things whatsoever ye would that men should do unto you, do ye even so to them." In Greek, in English or in any other tongue, it is a sentence whose thought is so precise and complete, whose movement is so rhythmical, whose ap-

---

[1] Read at the Congress of Religions in Buffalo, N. Y., June, 1901, and at the Peace Congress of the Churches, Glasgow, Scotland, September, 1901.

peal to the moral instincts is so direct, that one can scarcely hear it uttered without feeling the rising in his eye of an æsthetic tear. Thus is probably to be explained the fact that this great life principle, though so universally neglected and disobeyed, has been just as universally lauded.

The solemn and wonderful majesty of the Golden Rule, and likewise its everlasting verity and vitality, can be appreciated only when one looks carefully into the three elements which lie behind it and determine its formulation.

The first of these elements is the sense and understanding of justice which it assumes to exist in all men. One of the clearest things among human phenomena is the fact that men, not much matter how undeveloped, ignorant, or even wicked they may be, have a very clear knowledge of what is justice toward themselves. This sense manifests itself more often, perhaps, when injustice is done them. The Indian, for example, may be a wild, ignorant, violent son of the forest, but, standing face to face with the knowing white man, he comprehends very well how the latter ought to feel and act toward him.

Now the Golden Rule requires a man, with this clear sense of what ought to be done to himself, to set himself over into the place of the other man, and then do to the other man what he would have the

other man do to him if their personalities and places
were changed. The meaning is not, Do to others as
you would have them do to you in your present
position. Jesus Christ never uttered anything so
meaningless. The suppressed "If you were the
other man" gives the maxim its fine uniqueness
and supreme moral significance.

The second element in the rule is its assumption
that all men feel and know that others ought to love
them and fulfil toward them all the behests of love.
As I said was true in the matter of justice, it is just
as universal a fact in human phenomena that all men
desire others to appreciate and be kind to them, or,
in other words, to love them; and though they are
often ignorant of what real love ought to do, they
are quick, as a rule, to realise it when it comes from
a spirit of transparent good-will. The deeds of ill-
will they never require much time to fathom. The
Golden Rule thus, with its perfect ethical insight,
sets a man in other men's places, and exhorts him to
love them as he would be loved if he were they.

The third element is still more characteristic. It
insists that one's life of love and justice towards one's
fellows shall begin spontaneously with oneself, and
not after others have made the approaches. You must
take the initiative yourself without any thought of
how your action will be received, and you must live
in this spirit continually. You must be kind toward

the unthankful and the unjust. You must cause your sun to rise on the evil as on the good, and the rain of your outgoing goodness to fall on all men of all classes and conditions, as God does. If you love them only who love you, you may be a good Pharisee or a good anything-else that is dry and barren, but not a son of the Golden Rule.

One might well spend many hours, if there were time, in suggesting how the Golden Rule should be applied in the life of individuals, and what transformation in all human affairs would be brought about by its universal observance. It is generally believed that it ought to be observed by individuals in all their ordinary social relations, and that its high aim is not impossible of attainment. All men are particularly anxious that other people should keep it, though, of course, no one expects to observe it perfectly himself. A little leeway must be kept open for personal improvement!

Bad, however, as the world still is, as we all are, making plenty of occasion for sarcasm and irony when we talk about this golden maxim, I am convinced that in social life at the opening of this twentieth century, here and there in considerable sections of it, there is, in one form or another, much of real Golden Rule living. People are still a bit awkward about it, so novel is the experience, but the genuine article is found in many places. This is the supreme attainment of our civilisation, that men and women in considerable numbers now actually inhabit our planet whose lives are given to the service of others, who do as they would be done by. It is the most encouraging sign of the times that such numbers of people are talking Golden Rule and insisting on Golden Rule conduct — outside of church, I mean, in the storm and stress of daily life. In church of course everybody bows down to the Golden Rule, though many are careful to have the Golden Calf at hand, just outside the door, waiting for the after-service.

So much Golden Rule talk means much in the heart, for " out of the abundance of the heart the mouth speaketh." It indicates that there is a great Golden Rule revolution just before us in the social life of men, in the family, the church, the community; shall I say in business and in politics? Yes, in business and in politics also, for it will show itself there as soon, or nearly as soon, as anywhere else.

It is high time for all good men and women to begin to talk seriously about the Golden Rule in international affairs. These affairs have for various reasons become so conspicuous and potent in these days that they dominate nearly everything. Their influence for good or ill is felt everywhere, in religious and social circles, in business, at our very breakfast tables. The scale on which they are carried on is now so colossal that unless they can be thoroughly moralised and purified, the hope for the redemption of the world is not very great.

It has been and still is complacently assumed by many, one would not exaggerate much in saying by most people, that international affairs are a natural and hopeless anarchy, where every government may play the devil as much as it pleases; that it is impossible for a nation to live and prosper without ignoring and openly violating nearly every principle of the Golden Rule. Ambition, self-aggrandisement, outwitting other countries, belittling them, getting from them as much as possible with little or no return, exacting of them reparation for every least offence or wrong received, beating them in brutal combat, singing *Te Deums* over their defeat and humiliation, taking their country by conquest, reducing them to political slavery, annihilating their independence — this has been considered the mission, the duty, the glory of nations. Something of this conception still remains, so much of it, in fact, that it is difficult for any nation to escape its deadly fascination. Men are living whose actions indicate that they do not know that we have got beyond the days of Tamburlaine, who look upon the idea of love and good-will toward other nations as silly and contemptible nonsense, men to whom nothing but power and crushing force have any ultimate greatness and majesty.

But the growing spirit of our time repudiates all this. It demands something else, and will have something else. A nation is coming to be looked upon as only a larger social unit, subject to all the laws of conduct which govern men in their common social relations. A consciousness of universal humanity has appeared, and with it a corresponding conscience. The ordinary notions of national conduct are being everywhere challenged. It is openly urged by many teachers of public morality that the Golden Rule, which is the highest law, the only comprehensive law for individuals, is likewise the supreme law for nations, and that those governments which will not consent to observe it are guilty of great sin, and conspicuously dishonourable. More than this, there are now men and women in considerable numbers in many countries who steadily feel and act toward other lands as the Golden Rule dictates, and who take cheerfully any obloquy resulting therefrom.

This conception of national conduct is absolutely certain to prevail. It must be talked and written into the consciousness and the conscience of the world. Here lies our first international duty. We ought to promote international travel, international trade, religious, scientific, and literary fellowship between nations. But most of all, the peoples of the earth must be taught that it is their duty to feel and act toward one another as brethren and friends, and not as haters, thieves, robbers and cut-throats.

To say that the Golden Rule is inapplicable to nations is to reach the limit of moral absurdity, and to charge God with supreme folly. Ruskin once wrote: " I have met men who boldly said, ' There is no God,' but never till I began to move among English Christians did I ever conceive that men lived who with unblushing effrontery could say, ' There is a God, but He is a foolish God. He has put us under laws that are unworkable.' " God's Golden Rule is man's Golden Rule, wrought out, not in some far-away heaven, but here in the structure of man's individualistic and social nature; and it is just as workable between nations as between individuals, as any two nations would speedily find out which had the good sense and courage to put it to the test. Emerson once said that love as the basis of a State had never been tried, and that it was folly to say before the experiment had been made that it would not work. The Golden Rule has never been tried between nations, except in titbits possibly. We must insist that it have a full and fair trial; and until that time the sceptical croakers have no right to croak.

Nations have the same sense of what is just towards themselves as individuals have. No nation believes it right for another to make war upon it, to blockade its ports, to invade its territories, to kill off its young men, to break up its homes, to paralyse its industries, to reduce it to vassalage, to slice off its territory, or to extinguish its independence by force. No nation in our day believes it right for another to exclude its upright citizens of whatever class, to make their entrance into its borders and their residence there hard and annoying, or to interfere with its trade by exacting and crippling tariffs. No nation believes it right for another stronger than itself to lay upon it any demands, however small, which are dictated simply by superior might. What nation is there whose people believe it right for those of another to malign or ridicule them, to misrepresent their motives, to depreciate their manners and customs, and, in general, to belittle them? How sensitive nations are in all these respects to what justice demands toward themselves! The most elementary sense of fairness ought to lead them to do in all these matters as they would be done by, and any nation which does not do so is condemned, not by others, but by its own standards of right. If the nations half lived up to their light in this direction, there would not be half an hour's fighting among them in a century.

Going up to the higher plane, we find a similar state of affairs. Every nation desires to be appreciated and honoured by others, to have its people courteously and kindly treated when abroad, to have its institutions and customs respected and honoured, to have patience and charity shown towards its weaknesses and imperfections, and to have even its sins and wrongs treated in a merciful and forgiving spirit. In other words, all nations desire to be loved, spontaneously loved, by others, as truly and strongly as individuals ever do, and there is no more vanity in the national desire for appreciation than in the individual.

Here, then, we reach the high obligation of love between nation and nation. It lies in their very nature and relations to one another, and is not something that comes by imposition from without. A demand for respect and esteem imposes immediate obligation to give them to those from whom they are asked. There is no escape from this obligation without self-stultification and self-dishonour, of which nations and peoples have been all too guilty. " Thou shalt love thy neighbour as thyself " signifies, when translated into international speech, Thou shalt love the neighbouring nation — every nation, that is, according to the interpretation of the Great Teacher — as thou lovest thy own, thou, the government, thou, the citizen. Thou shalt seek its good, its prosperity, its honour; thou shalt respect its liberties, its rights, its individuality; thou shalt promote its progress in knowledge, in industry, in commerce, in happiness, in spiritual life; thou shalt be merciful towards its sins and forgiving towards its trespasses.

In attempting to get a right conception of the true friendship which should exist between the peoples and nations of the earth, one must beware of taking too much stock in that governmental chumminess whose aim is chiefly mutual support in carrying out schemes of greed and aggression. At the bottom of this always lurks more or less dislike of other peoples, and usually sinister designs against them. There is nothing whatever of the Golden Rule in triple or dual alliances of the ordinary type, nor in those effusive promises of support in possible, mysteriously hinted-at conflicts by which one government tries to secure a powerful friend in another, to aid it in some meanness which it is accomplishing. The Golden Rule knows no race or hemisphere. One must beware also of taking for the genuine article of which we are talking that sentimental frothing which so often takes place at diplomatic banquets and international dinners where everlasting friendship is pledged between the countries whose high dignitaries are swallowing viands and drinking champagne side by side, all of which loud-mouthed pledges are forgotten before the stars set. To call this international love and friendship is to show an utter lack of wits.

The observance of the two duties of international justice and international love in even a modest measure would put an end forever to war, which is totally irreconcilable with the demands of either. War is the negation of both love and justice. It is the apotheosis of selfishness, hate and brute force. But it would do more than put an end to war. It would bring the nations into mutual confidence and trust, into intelligent and sympathetic coöperation for the promotion of the real interests of each and all. This is the positive and nobler side of peace, which so many of its opponents fail to grasp. They take it for a mere negative thing, equivalent to social idleness and stagnation. Toward this noble state of international coöperation in all high endeavour the abolition of war is only an important step. Toward its attainment is demanded just as imperatively the abolition of a number of other international wickednesses, with which war is so closely allied and out of which it inevitably springs. The axe must be laid at the root of the whole tree.

Who shall begin the application of the Golden Rule to international affairs? What nation? I said that the Golden Rule requires one to take the initiative oneself in putting it into practice, without waiting to see what others will do. Theoretically, all the nations ought to begin together, at once. As Americans, as Englishmen, as Frenchmen, as Germans, we ought to insist, so far as our influence extends, that our own nations begin at once to live out the Golden Rule toward other nations in a much higher and wider sense than they have yet done, and that they abandon forthwith every ambition and every policy inconsistent with this supreme law of life. If the nations refuse to do this, we must do it ourselves as individuals at every point where our lives touch the larger life of the world. The men and women who are here to-day are powerful enough, few as they are, to work a very great transformation in the thought and conduct of their nations in this respect within a comparatively brief time, if in thought, speech and conduct they were perpetually true, in the circles in which they move, to the Golden Rule ideals and laws of life.

Many people shudder at the thought of trusting the life and destinies of the nation to the protection of the simple moral defences of a course of conduct strictly in harmony with the principles of the maxim which we are considering. They frighten themselves with the fancy that a nation that was always just and loving, that lived for other nations in the spirit of self-sacrifice, that therefore discarded and refused to employ in its defence the weapons whose use always means death and desolation to others, would immediately be pounced upon by others and destroyed. As for myself, so profound is my faith in the conquering and preserving power of such life and conduct as that of which I have been speaking, that I would not hesitate an instant to stake the existence, the prosperity and the honour of my country upon it. Indeed, I do not believe that any nation will ever be entirely secure in either its existence or its prosperity until it abandons reliance on all other defences, and trusts itself completely and in good faith to a life of justice and self-sacrificing love. It is selfish ambition and its handmaid, brute force, which have been the cause of the downfall of every nation which has perished in the past. Might has proved itself unworthy of confidence a thousand times over, even in the defence of righteous causes. It is proving itself so again in these days when heaven and earth are ransacked to find means to make the strong arm stronger. In the simple name of reason and good sense, it is time to abandon the shield and sword and to trust to the loving heart and the helpful hand.

If I believed, as I do not, that the adoption of the Golden Rule as the law of its life and conduct would leave the nation to be preyed upon and destroyed, I should still not hesitate to advise its adoption. If the nation died thus, it would bless the world infinitely more by its death than it could possibly do by a life, however long, filled with selfish ambition and disregard of others. I should not be in the least ashamed to be a citizen of a nation which gave its life in this lofty and disinterested way. On the contrary, I should be ashamed of any country of which I was a citizen which tried to save its life and exalt its honour by crushing the life and liberties of any people, or in any way doing them harm. Men have given their lives for holy causes and been honoured for evermore. Why should not a nation do so, if the pathway of duty led to the cross? The author of the Golden Rule gave up His life in the effort to set up the kingdom of heaven among men and to save the world. Why should it be thought a thing dishonourable and unworthy for a nation to sacrifice itself to promote that kingdom and to assist in completing the redemption of the race? Is it glorious for men to die in self-sacrifice for others, and ignoble for a nation? No! There is one supreme law of love and self-sacrifice for both, leading always to life and honour, though sometimes by way of suffering and death.

THE NATION'S RESPONSIBILITY
FOR PEACE [1]

A NATION's responsibility for making and keeping peace, in its relations to other nations, is the same as that of the individual in his relations to others. There is not one moral law for men and another for nations. The principles which ought to govern the life and conduct of the one are equally obligatory in the case of the other. The moral law is as unbending, the conscience as imperative when a man voluntarily compounds his deeds with those of other men as when he acts alone. Whatever in principle is a crime for a man is a crime for a nation.

Individuals are under obligation, according to accessible light, to accept and to follow the moral law of right, and the Christian law of love. Nothing else dare be asserted of nations. The Golden Rule spans the seas and reaches across national frontiers as well as over the distances which separate individual men. It is a radically false position that a nation

---

[1] Delivered at the New England Convention of the National Reform Association held in Boston, February. 1895.

exists for itself alone, for the exclusive good of its own people. It exists for others as for itself. The law of love and of self-sacrifice is an essential part, is indeed the very highest part of the expression of its outgoing life. No nation, therefore, can rightly be called Christian which does not, in its relations to all other peoples, follow this law. If it be impossible, as has been asserted in prominent quarters, to found and conduct a State on the principles contained in the sermon on the mount, then no Christian nation can ever exist. From all this it follows that positive peace-making, not peace-keeping merely but the effort to bring the peoples of the earth to a permanent state of peace and harmonious coöperation, is the very highest of the nation's obligations.

The responsibility of a nation rests upon its geographical position and limits; its intellectual and moral enlightenment; its power of exerting influence, whether this be material, intellectual or moral; its religious, social and political ideals and purposes; and its general historic character and development. Looked at from these various standpoints, it will be easily seen that responsibility for the creation and maintenance of the peace of the world rests upon the United States as upon no other country.

Our country is predestined by its geographical position and extent to be the peace-maker of the world; it ought to give all diligence to make its calling and election sure. With the exception of the northern and about half of the southern frontier (and the exception is of no great importance) we have no border line connecting us with other nations. The wide seas intervene. This separation naturally relieves us of many of the complications and anxieties which arise from close proximity. It tends to make us a quiet, peace-loving, peace-seeking, unarmed people. This has been its practical effect. It has been difficult to maintain a militia on our soil. No effort has ever been made to have much of a standing army, and our navy, about which we have been most tempted to sin, has led a precarious existence. It is true that by reason of the cable and the swifter-growing ships we are constantly getting nearer to other countries and are in increasing danger of losing the peaceful spirit which our isolation has had much to do with creating. But the isolation can never be wholly overcome and will continue to exert a benign influence.

Though set apart we have been set in a large and goodly place. We have no excuse for coveting any nation's climate or soil or productions. We have these in a variety nowhere else known. We need not fret ourselves into a fighting spirit by seeking an outlet by sea to the rest of the world, as Russia is doing on the east and the west, for all the paths of the oceans are open to us. With thirteen thousand miles of seacoast, we need not envy any nation a few island stations. God, in his geographic and historic providences, has thus set us apart that he might build up among the nations of the earth one with a new spirit, and thus lead the world to peace. We may thwart his purposes by selfishness, narrowness, fear and the wish to be like the armor-clad peoples across the water, but we cannot do this without basely trampling under our feet his clearly expressed intentions as to our destiny.

Our responsibility arising from intellectual and moral enlightenment is very great. We are fond of talking about our great public school system and the privileges of a common education which it gives to all citizens. Higher education is well developed among us for a comparatively large proportion of our youth. Making proper allowance for national buncombe from which the most of us suffer more or less, we may safely assert that intellectual enlightenment for the people as a whole is considerably greater in the United States than in any other part of the world. Morally our responsibility is still larger. No other nation, with possibly one exception, has had such a schooling in Christian morals. The Bible has been our text-book in practical ethics. Fifty millions of our people, however poorly they may have profited from its instruction, have been in contact with it from their childhood. I have been repeatedly told, on the continent of Europe, by thoughtful men, that it is the Bible which has made us a great people. It has certainly made us a responsible people. The sermon on the mount is the moral light according to which it is our national duty to walk. Neither the people, nor Congresses, nor Cabinets, nor Presidents can be excused in the least from this high obligation.

Passing to the power to exert influence, the United States here certainly stands alone. Her great extent and variety of territory; her population already nearly double in size that of any other civilized country, if we exclude Russia from the list; her vast wealth and inexhaustible resources; her general intellectual enlightenment and moral and religious advantages; the character of her civil and political institutions — all these invest her with a tremendous power of influencing the world's destinies. If the American people were as quick to recognize the exceptional responsibilities imposed by this peculiar position of influence as they are to pride themselves on the reputation which it is supposed to bring, our spread-eagleism would all die and our already fairly commendable zeal to promote the good of the world would be enlarged into an earnest, united, persistent and heroic effort, along all lines, to bring the family of nations to realize the highest attainable ideal of brotherhood and mutual helpfulness.

Looking a little closer, we find that much of our responsibility arises from our professed religious, social and political ideals and purposes. What a nation intelligently and conscientiously professes to be determines in no small measure what it ought to do. In religion, we are built on freedom of conscience. Church and State have no connection. The Christian people group themselves into religious organizations according to their preferences. According to our theory no man can be forced to be a Christian, or hindered in the least from becoming one. Socially, we are built on simple manhood. We profess to have no caste, no class distinctions either temporary or permanent. Our social circles and groups form and break up according to individual preferences, pursuits and conveniences. Our political claims are freedom and self-government, equality of right and privilege for all before the law. These great religious, social and political principles faithfully carried out naturally lead to peace, for peace always follows in the footsteps of liberty. Furthermore they are a proclamation of peace in advance. Whoever announces that he will live by them declares his purpose to live in peace with his fellow-men. Our nation in founding itself on these principles has renounced forever the supposed right of conquest. It has declared in the most solemn manner that it will treat with justice, and respect the rights of, every other nation, however weak and defenceless; that it will do as it would be done by; that it will abstain from every sort of open or covert interference with the affairs of others. The rôle which by the nature of our institutions we have assumed before the world has laid upon us the high obligation to manifest straightforwardness, kindness and forbearance in all our foreign affairs. "A spirited foreign policy," in the usual sense of the expression, is utterly unworthy of a nation into whose whole structure are built the principles of freedom and equal rights.

How has the nation met its responsibility?

Though there are dark spots here and there and plenty of guilt for low motives and bad spirit, yet there is much in the record of the one hundred eight years since the creation of the constitution of which no one need be ashamed. Of international wars we have had only three in all that time, and these combined covered a period of less than five years. The war of 1812 lasted two and a half years and was a piece of international misfortune quite as much as of international crime. An ocean cable would certainly have prevented it. The light of history shows that the American sin of impatience and hot-headedness was quite as much the cause of the war as the British sin of impressment. It was condemned by many of our citizens at the time, especially in New England, and very few well-read people can now be found who justify it. The little war with Algiers lasted only a few weeks and has been practically forgotten. The two years war with Mexico was chargeable to the crime of slavery, and is now universally condemned. At the time many of the best citizens of the country were amazed and indignant at the government's folly in entering into it. Lowell, writing of the war at the time, in the Biglow papers, said:

> *Ez fer war, I call it murder, —*
> *There you hev it plain an' flat;*
> *I don't want to go no furder*
> *Than my Testyment fer that.*

We have had, then, in our history more than one hundred years of peace with other nations and less than five years of war, and we have had the national honesty and conscientiousness to confess in considerable measure our guilt in connection with these five years. This is no mean record.

The peace of the world has been powerfully promoted also by our union of States and by the Supreme Court which constitutes in reality a great inter-state tribunal, of the same type, in many respects, as that which it is proposed to establish for the nations of the world. It is true that the light of this union went nearly out during the bloody days of the civil war. This war, one of the wickedest in the history of the world, was the inevitable outcome of the monstrous crime of slavery, of which the whole nation, not the South only, was deeply guilty. The guilt of the war was the guilt of slavery, which was a concrete and wholesale denial of every principle of liberty and free government, a huge national lie, which came back to scorch and blister the lips that uttered it. But in spite of these dark and horrible years, whose fruits we are still reaping, the union of the States which began with the first federation of the colonies has gone steadily on until it has built itself into a massive structure extending from ocean to ocean, whose two chief pillars are entire local self-government and complete national union and coöperation. The result of this union has been, with the exception mentioned, an unbroken and ever deepening peace. Differences between the States, where there have been any (there have been almost none), have gone to the Supreme Court and there been settled with less difficulty than differences between individuals in the ordinary courts of law. The United States of North America is the prefiguration and the first historical exemplification of what is some time, in some form, to be the United States of the world, the result of which shall be universal and perpetual peace.

Our theory that a man of any land has a right to choose his home wherever he can find one and change it as often as he pleases has done much to break down international prejudices and exclusiveness, and thus prepare the way for peace. Up to the beginning of this century it was held that a man owed perpetual allegiance to the country in which he was born. This theory of slavery to country the United States has destroyed. Whoever becomes a naturalized citizen of this country ceases to owe any allegiance to his native land, whether he be at home or on the remotest foreign shore. The same is true of an American who chooses to adopt the citizenship of another country. By opening our citizenship to people of all lands we have proclaimed aloud the brotherhood and essential equality of right and privilege of all men.

The influence of this doctrine and practice in breaking down hostilities between the nations and bringing them into closer sympathy with each other can not be overestimated. It is painful to have to record that we have in a very wicked way belied our own teaching in our treatment of one or two peoples, notably of the Chinese, but this bit of national folly and iniquity we shall soon get over.

The United States has likewise nobly met its

responsibility for peace by arbitrating nearly all of its difficulties with foreign countries, by acting as arbitrator between other nations and by using its good offices to bring other governments to adjust their conflicts by peaceful means. Over against the three wars mentioned above we are able to set thirty-seven cases in which our country has settled important differences with other nations by arbitration, nearly as many as all other countries combined can show. In nearly a dozen instances the President of the United States has been called upon to act as arbitrator for other powers, and in recent years our ambassadors, ministers and consuls have been doing much to promote peace in all quarters of the globe.

In view of the historic record which the nation has thus made and the character which it has built up before the world, it must be confessed that its responsibility stands much higher to-day than ever before. The responsibility is further heightened by the fact that the old world is just now possessed by an unaccountable military mania which is pushing the nations on to financial ruin and to a social and political cataclysm whose disastrous consequences, unless prevented in some way, can be only dimly guessed. If a nation was ever needed to stand up as a bulwark against militarism, it is at the present hour. There is none but ours to do this. The rest have gone too far wrong already. Will our country do its duty? Will it stand by its historic character and record, or will it allow itself to be carried away with the general flood of senseless rivalry in war preparation? It is too early yet to answer the question fully. What the answer will have to be is certain if the present movement for the universal introduction of military instruction into the public schools and the movement for a forced militia service in the States come to realization. We can not yet believe that these movements will be allowed to accomplish their purpose. Opposition to them is growing throughout the country as their real significance becomes known. They are so thoroughly un-American, so fraught with danger to our civil and religious liberties, that the people ought to rise up in common accord and stop them. We do not conceal from ourselves that there is imminent danger from them, and we raise our voice in solemn protest against them as unworthy of our country, as contradictory to the spirit of our institutions, and therefore as unpatriotic.

It has been seriously proposed to increase our standing army. There is not the shadow of an excuse for doing this, as is clear from the fact that each advocate of it gives a different reason for doing it. Of this increase to any serious extent there is no immediate danger, though it will be the necessary outcome of military extension if undertaken along other lines.

In the matter of the navy we are going steadily astray and no one can prophesy where the evil will stop. Now that the work has been commenced, the war spirits, the alarmists, the imitators among us will never be satisfied until the United States navy is as large as that of England, and then the cry will be raised, as it is now continually raised in England, that we must have a fleet of war-ships twice as numerous as that of any other nation. If our greatness and glory, if our national defences are to be found along this line, then we must go to the front at whatever cost. Do the people want this? Will they permit it?

If I had the ear of my country, a country of whose record, in spite of her faults, every citizen has a right to be proud, I should say, unhesitatingly, that we ought to move in exactly the opposite direction. The more nearly unarmed we shall be, the more respected, the stronger and the safer we shall be. The great problem of the world to-day is international reconciliation, the arrest of militarism, disarmament. God by unmistakable providences has appointed us to lead in the solution. We can never cure the evil by taking part in it. We should dare to do our duty and then trust in God, as we profess to do. We ought not, therefore, to build another war vessel.

We already have enough to serve as symbols of power, to create all the friction necessary between us and other peoples. It is undeniable that we were never more secure, never more respected, never more prosperous and happy than when twenty years ago our navy consisted largely of a lot of rotting hulks. The alarmists may explain this fact as they will, but they cannot deny it. The time of international aggression is almost entirely gone by. Conscience and mutual respect between nations stand for something now. No nation has the least disposition to attack us; quite the contrary. No nation would think of attacking us, if we had not one single war-ship, not one coast-defence gun. If we should begin in our small way the work of disarmament, we should thereby build up, in the respect thus created for us among other nations, a national defence greater than has ever been possessed by any land. Do not think me jesting, or playing with simple fancies. What I say I take for one of the soberest of the sober truths. It is always safe to stake the destiny of a nation on what is right.

We stand at this hour of our national life at the parting of the ways. Calling us from one direction comes the sound of the martial drum beat, the shout of gathering armies, the siren song of the " pomp and circumstance " of war, the clang of the armor-clad old world, the cry of the wounded and dying past, the voices of fear and distrust which fly to bayonets and cannon for defence. From the other road comes the call of love and truth, of spiritual freedom, of civil and religious liberty; the voice of our national destiny, of peace and good-will and human brotherhood; the voice of the happy and trustful future; the voice of the Prince of Peace.

Which way shall we turn our feet?

INTERNATIONAL ARBITRATION
AT THE OPENING OF THE
TWENTIETH CENTURY [1]

INTERNATIONAL arbitration is a comparatively modern thing, belonging almost entirely to the period commencing with the opening of the nineteenth century. The arbitrations before that time were for the most part between individuals, communities, different branches of the same dynasty, or between vassal states and feudal chiefs, rather than between nations in our modern sense of the term. This method of settling difficulties between peoples came about with the decline of despotism and the growth of political liberty, and the consequent development and realization of the idea of nationality in its modern sense. Nations, in the sense of free and independent peoples, whose unity is natural and voluntary, and who observe in a measure the limits which have been marked out for them by the providence of God in the geographic structure of the earth and in the historic development of races, did not exist in any permanent way much more than a

---

[1] Reprinted from the *Advocate of Peace*, April, 1905.

hundred years ago. The movement toward settled
and self-governed nations, which has resulted in
the building up and compacting of this great Republic and in the unification of Great Britain, of
France, of Italy, of Germany, and of other nations
in both hemispheres to a greater or less extent, grew
out of the many liberating and civilizing forces
which have been playing on society since the beginning of the Christian era, to go no farther back,
and with it has come sufficient international respect
and unselfishness, a sufficient sense of the mutual
interdependence of nations, to make arbitration not
only possible but natural and inevitable. So long as
feudalism remained, international arbitration was
impossible, because there were really no nations to
arbitrate. Even after the nations were somewhat
settled in their proper boundaries, so long as they
were ruled by men whose despotic and world-
grasping spirit led them year after year into schemes
for the subjection of other peoples, international
arbitration in any general and settled way was still
impossible. With the fall of Napoleon, in whom this
spirit found its final embodiment, the old order of
things was broken and the new began to appear.

Arbitration implies independent and mutually
respecting parties standing over against each other,
with difficulties which they cannot settle themselves,

because of the strong feeling which each has that he is in the right and that he cannot therefore yield to the other's view. It also implies a conviction that there is a better and more rational, or at least a safer and less expensive, way of settling difficulties than that of fighting like brutes about them. It further implies confidence in the fairness and good sense of one's fellow-men, who may be called in to take the dispute and sit down with it in the impartial court of reason and say how it shall be adjusted.

It may easily be seen, therefore, why arbitration, though it may have taken place frequently between individuals and small bodies of men, could not, in the moral state of society then existing, have occurred much on an international scale prior to the opening of the nineteenth century. Not a little of the spirit of unrespecting selfishness and greed of the past centuries still lingers, and numberless jealousies and ill-feelings left behind by former aggressions and acts of injustice have rendered arbitration, until comparatively recently, much less frequent than it ought to have been; but its appearance in the nineteenth century in many important cases is a proof that not only individual men but the nations in their dealings one with another have got a good deal above the brute and have begun to be largely and generously human.

Before a detailed analysis of the arbitration movement during the past century is given, attention should be called a little more specifically to what arbitration in a simpler and narrower way accomplished in the past; for the present movement is not alone the outgrowth of Christian civilization in general, but also of the arbitrations themselves which are scattered along through the previous centuries. The movement has a purely human and rational side, so that even among pagan nations and before the Christian era cases of this mode of settling disputes are recorded, and many others doubtless occurred which have passed into oblivion. The madness and insanity of war did not always prevail. There were lucid moments when the real human nature temporarily asserted itself. Two sons of Darius settled the question of the succession to the throne by arbitration. Cyrus sought the good offices of a prince of India to end a dispute between him and the King of Assyria. In the Greek civilization, where the state was everything and love of country an all-absorbing passion, cases of arbitration between Greek and Greek were not infrequent, though no Greek state seems ever to have arbitrated with a foreign country. In these the Amphictyonic Councils, famous sages, victors in the games and especially the Oracle at Delphi were the arbitrators. The system of law and of law courts, in which the citizens of a country determine their questions by a forced litigation under the power of the civil authorities, has its root in practically the same principles as arbitration. In the Roman empire this system prevailed, and the simpler method of voluntary arbitration was not much known.

When Christianity came with its doctrine of love and human brotherhood, arbitration became a frequent and probably the usual method by which difficulties between individual Christians were settled. The reader will remember Paul's passionate appeal to the Corinthians in behalf of this simple Christian method as against the forced and selfish litigations in the law courts.

In later times the bishops trials became a fixed institution among Christians. If the history of these Christian settlements by arbitration could be written, it would take a very large library to contain the accounts of them. They have been numerous through all the Christian centuries, and are still frequent in our own time. Not a year has passed, it may be safely asserted, since the first organization of Christian societies, in which many a bishop, minister or wise Christian layman, either alone or with others, has not by arbitration or mediation adjusted differences between brethren. The practice thus created and fostered by Christian love and forbearance has largely leavened the whole of society with

its influence, and its reasonableness is now nearly
universally recognized, even where temporary gusts
of passion or hereditary prejudices prevent its employment in particular cases. It is on this basis of
Christian principle and practice, running back to the
days of the Prince of Peace, that the whole structure
of modern international arbitration rests.

What was found so useful and practicable among
individuals was naturally seen to be just as capable
of successful application to groups and communities
of men, and it began early to be so applied. Private
war, the great curse of the middle ages, was banished from European society only after the application to it of arbitration and arbitration courts.
Feudalism had spread this evil everywhere. Chal-
lenges to battle were made for the most trivial and
absurd causes. A state of almost utter lawlessness
came to prevail, and strife and bloodshed were perpetual. Religious sentiment was invoked against the
evil. The clergy preached peace. Men went from
village to village proclaiming it in the name of
Christ. Great councils were held to promote it. The
popes sent out encyclicals in its behalf. The " Peace
of God " was proclaimed, and certain days, places
and callings were placed under the protection of its
sheltering wing. Religious fraternities or peace associations to reconcile enemies were formed. Pledges
of peace were administered to the fierce barons over

holy relics. But the tide of hatred and of blood surged on. Finally, as a last remedy, when all the efforts put forth for nearly two centuries against the evil seemed about to end in failure, courts of arbitration were formed by the barons, the nobles, the bishops and the cities, and for two centuries and more were applied from time to time to the settlement of the almost endless misunderstandings and quarrels of the time. In this way private war was ultimately banished from society.

From the beginning of the sixteenth to the opening of the nineteenth century we have the great war movements of nationalities — aggression, bloodshed and desolation on a colossal scale. The feudal lords are replaced by kings and emperors in whom the old feudal spirit still lives. Private war with its everlasting bickerings and its petty troops of galloping dragoons and murderous squads of footmen gives place to war between sovereigns and whole peoples, with their great generals, their large armies, their deep-seated hatreds and their craftily laid plans of territorial extension. No sooner are national boundaries marked off than they are disturbed. The map of Europe changes with nearly every campaign. " I saw," said Grotius, writing at this time, " throughout all Christendom a readiness to make war which would cause the very barbarians to blush for shame."

England, France, Prussia, Austria, Spain, Italy, the Netherlands, were almost continuous battlefields on which the sound of the cannon was always heard and the blood never ceased to flow. This long, gloomy period of international aggression and crime — the age of Charles the Fifth, of Henry the Eighth, of Bloody Mary, of Frederick the Great, of Charles the Twelfth, of Louis the Fourteenth, of Napoleon the First; the age of the Inquisition and of the French Revolution; the age of the Seven Years War, of the Thirty Years War, or rather the age of perpetual war — reached its culmination at the opening of the nineteenth century in the Napoleonic campaigns which ended at Waterloo. Then a reaction came. The common conscience began to revolt at the sight of human beings forever devouring one another and of selfish, haughty sovereigns treading down and destroying all the most sacred rights and interests of men.

The first steps of this revolt had been taken in the seventeenth century. Christian conviction had become such and Christian principles had so influenced thought that the war system began to be attacked at its very roots. It was declared to be both unchristian and unreasonable. Hugo Grotius, the great Dutch jurist and theologian, who laid the foundations of the modern juridic movement against war, attacked it particularly on the latter ground. He declared that war was a cruel and unsatisfactory method, that its horrors should be mitigated and that arbitration should be substituted for it as far as practicable in the settlement of difficulties. He expounded his doctrine with so much erudition and force that he deeply affected the thought of Europe, and laid the foundation of a better international law. Publicists took up the problem which he had raised. The law of nations was unfolded and emphasized. Projects for universal peace were drawn up. Locke, Kant, Penn, Pufendorf, Vattel, Montesquieu, Bentham and others drew up schemes which have had a powerful influence on thought ever since. Lessing and Herder put the new ideas into verse. The foundations of the modern movement were likewise laid deep in the religious sentiment by Menno Simons, by George Fox, and later by John Wesley.

Soon after the opening of the nineteenth century the movement against war took on an organized and definitive form. This organized movement growing out of these historic preparations and coming as a revolt against the bloody régime of the three preceding centuries, followed two lines of development, one sentimental, the other juridic. The sentimental, or that for the awakening and education of public sentiment against war, manifested itself during the nineteenth century in the organization of peace societies, in sermons and public lectures, in literary productions, through the press, through international congresses and conferences, through public manifestos and memorials to governments; the juridic, or that for the creation of legal remedies for war, expressed itself in improved diplomacy, in attempts to reform international law, in arbitration and in efforts for the establishing of permanent treaties of arbitration and a permanent international tribunal. These two lines of movement, one of which is just as important as the other, have been interlaced at every stage and have grown strong together. The culmination of the arbitration side of the movement in actual practice during the last decade and a half has been very remarkable, as is now well known.

The Jay Treaty of 1794, between the United States and Great Britain, provided for the settlement of three questions by mixed commissions. The first of these commissions, appointed to determine what river was meant by the St. Croix in the treaty of 1783, rendered its decision in 1798. The second commission failed to render a decision, and the matter of British claims referred to it was settled by treaty in 1802. The third commission, appointed to determine the loss suffered by American vessels at the hands of Great Britain during the war between that country and France, closed its labors in 1804.

These settlements by mixed commissions were not formal arbitrations, though they were essentially so. The method of adjusting disputes by joint commissions has continued in vogue up to the present time, and no less than three hundred controversies between nations have in this way been disposed of since the beginning of the nineteenth century. Many of these were questions of claims, but some of them, like the Alaska boundary dispute, were controversies of the first importance.

The Treaty of Ghent, December 24, 1814, provided for the formal arbitration of three questions between the United States and Great Britain. The first of these referred to certain islands in the Passamaquoddy Bay, and was decided by commissioners in 1817. The solution of the second question, that of the north-eastern boundary of the United States, was attempted by commissioners in 1816. They failed to agree, and in 1827 the question was referred to the King of the Netherlands, whose decision, in 1831, was waived by both governments, and the matter was finally settled by compromise. The third question, that of the northern boundary of the United States along the Great Lakes, was partially settled by commissioners in 1822, and finished in 1842 by treaty. These commissions had an umpire, and the settlements were therefore formal arbitrations. Similar settlements of claims by arbitral com-

missions were made at this early period between the
United States and Spain, and between France and
Russia.

Since the time of the Treaty of Ghent, 1814,
about two hundred sixty international controversies have been settled by arbitration, or an average of about three a year for the whole period of
ninety years. More than sixty of these were in the
decade from 1890 to 1900, and sixty of them have
occurred since the twentieth century opened. So
common has the practice of arbitration become in
recent years that cases are nowadays constantly
pending between some of the nations, there being
several at the present time. The United States has
been a party to over sixty of these settlements; Great
Britain to more than seventy; while fifteen of the
cases have been between these two English-speaking
nations alone. France, Spain, Portugal, Germany,
Italy, Holland, Denmark, Belgium, Russia, Greece,
Turkey, Switzerland, Japan, Afghanistan, Persia,
China, Morocco, Mexico and Liberia have each
been parties to one or more of these settlements,
France, with over thirty cases, coming next to the
United States and Great Britain. All of the South
American and Central American States except two
or three have had arbitrations.

It is to be noticed that along with these cases adjusted by arbitration must be placed a large number

settled by diplomacy, many of which would formerly have produced war. Many modern diplomats have been in the truest sense of the term peacemakers, and have not only prevented war, but the necessity even of arbitration.

The nations referred to as having taken part in these pacific settlements — some thirty-seven of them all told — cover a large part of the habitable portion of the globe, and include a considerable number of countries not usually thought to be much civilized.

The cases referred to cover nearly every sort of question with which nations have to deal in their relations to one another — questions of boundary and violation of territory, of trespasses committed and injuries received in time of war, of the murder of citizens of one country by those of another, of disputed sovereignty over islands, questions of protectorates, of seizure of ships, of interference with commerce, of fisheries. Some of the controversies have been the occasion of diplomatic correspondence carried on for months, sometimes for years, by some of the ablest statesmen of modern times. In some instances, after diplomacy had exhausted its resources, the cases were dropped for a time, only to be taken up again and finally referred to disinterested parties. Large sums of money have been involved in a number of the disputes, no less than

$22,000,000 having changed hands in the three cases between the United States and Great Britain in 1871. The sense of national dignity and honor has often been keenly touched in the earlier stages of the controversies, and the newspapers on both sides have not infrequently tried to kindle the flame of war.

All these difficulties, though of exactly the same kind as those which in former times resulted speedily in disastrous and often long-continued wars, have, however, finally been settled with no great delay, with a trifling outlay of money, and without the least injury to the self-respect or honor of any country involved. The decisions have, with one or two trifling exceptions, been accepted cheerfully and faithfully carried out, and not the shadow of a war-cloud has ever been produced by one of them. On the contrary, the result has nearly invariably been increased mutual respect and a greater willingness to coöperate in all practicable ways for the common good.

For many years past the number of difficulties settled by arbitration has greatly exceeded the number of international controversies which have led to war, and the rule of the past has become the exception of the present. But one war makes more fuss in the world and gets more notice in the newspapers than a hundred arbitrations. These arbitration settlements have taken place so noiselessly and with so little public excitement that the ordinary well-read citizen could not name more than three or four out of the whole number, and the real triumphs of the principle are therefore only vaguely and imperfectly realized. Arbitration as a method of settling international controversies has already won its case and justified itself at the bar of human reason, and has become, as Mr. David Dudley Field said in the last paper but one that he ever wrote, a recognized part of the public law of the civilized nations.

The crowning event of the nineteenth century in the matter of arbitration, an event which grew out of the whole work of the century, was the establishment, at its close, of the Permanent International Court at The Hague. Such a court of arbitration had been advocated from the second decade of the century by the Peace Societies, and later by the International Law Association, the Peace Congresses, the Interparliamentary Union, national and local bar associations, special arbitration conferences, church assemblies, women's organizations, and others.

The Rescript of the Czar of Russia which brought about the Conference at The Hague was issued on the 24th of August, 1898. The Conference met on the 18th of May, 1899, under the auspices of the Netherlands government. It was composed of one hundred delegates sent by twenty-six nations, including all the first-class powers of the world. It sat until the 29th day of July. It was called more particularly to consider the question of a possible reduction of the armaments and the war budgets of the nations. It found itself unable to do anything important in this direction, and in response to the multiplied appeals which came to it from Western Europe and America, it took up the subject of a permanent system of arbitration, and at its close signed, with two other conventions, the Convention for the Pacific Settlement of International Disputes. This convention, in addition to providing for special mediation to prevent war and for commissions of inquiry in cases of difference where the facts were in dispute, made provision for the creation of a Permanent International Court of Arbitration, which should be open, for the adjudication of disputes, to all the signatory powers, and to any others that might subsequently be permitted to become parties to the convention.

Within two years a sufficient number of the signatories had ratified the convention to put it into effect, and in April, 1901, the Court was declared by the Netherlands Minister of Foreign Affairs to be properly organized and ready for business. The Convention was finally ratified by all the signatory

powers except China, Turkey, Persia and Monte-
negro, and when the second Hague Conference met
the total number of members of the Court was
seventy-six, each of the signatory powers being
authorized by the Convention to appoint not to
exceed four.

The Court, after some studied neglect by certain
powers, was put into successful operation by the
United States and Mexico by the reference to it, in
May, 1902, of the controversy about the Pious
Fund of the Californias, which had been long pending between the two countries. The case was argued
in September and October of that year by counsel of
the two governments before the tribunal of five
members chosen from the Court, and at the end
of four weeks the award, sustaining the contention of
the United States, was rendered. The expenses of
the trial were small. The judgment of the Court
was cheerfully accepted by the Mexican government, the amount of the claims paid, and the controversy passed out of existence.

This auspicious opening of the Permanent International Court of Arbitration was followed by the
reference to it the following year of the controversy
which arose in connection with the Venezuela
trouble as to whether the three powers which had
used force against Venezuela in an effort to collect
debts due their citizens should have preference over

the pacific creditors in the payment of these claims from the revenues from two ports which had been set apart for this purpose. In this famous case eleven of the powers of the world were contestants before the Court. The decision of the tribunal, which consisted of three members chosen from the Court, was rendered after long and patient deliberation. It was a surprise and disappointment to many of the friends of peace, but it was loyally accepted by all the powers concerned.

Before the opening of the second Hague Conference two other disputes — the House Tax Case between Japan on the one hand and Great Britain, France and Germany on the other, and the question of the protectorate of France over the Sultan of Muscat, to which Great Britain and France were parties — were referred to the Court and happily disposed of.

It will thus be seen that the permanent International Tribunal for the adjustment of differences between the nations was organized and entered successfully on its great career much sooner than even the most sanguine had a decade ago dared to hope.

But the work done in its organization, immensely important as it was, was an incomplete one. Not all the nations of the world were parties to the Convention, and none of them were pledged by treaty stipulations to submit controversies to the jurisdiction of the newly organized tribunal. An attempt to remedy the first defect was made at the second Pan-American Conference held at Mexico City in the winter of 1901–02. The important work of this conference was done along the line of arbitration. All the states of the Western Hemisphere signed by their representatives in that gathering a protocol declaring their adherence to the Hague Conventions, and the United States and Mexico were authorized to take the necessary steps for the opening of these conventions to them. A second protocol signed at Mexico City provided for the obligatory reference of all questions of claims to the arbitration of the Hague Court.

The second defect in the constitution of the Hague Court, if defect it may be called, it has been sought to remedy by securing the conclusion of special treaties of obligatory arbitration between the nations two and two or in groups. This movement has culminated with surprising and encouraging rapidity.

Previously to the setting up of the Hague Court all efforts to secure treaties of arbitration between nations had failed. As early as 1883 the Swiss government had approached our own with this end in view, but nothing came of it. The general treaty of arbitration for the American republics drafted at the first Pan-American Conference in 1889–1890 lapsed and was never ratified. Ten years of earnest effort for an arbitration treaty between Great Britain and the United States ended in the signing of the Olney-Pauncefote treaty at the opening of 1897. This treaty also failed in the United States Senate. The same year a general treaty of arbitration was negotiated between Italy and the Argentine Republic, but it never went into effect.

The labor spent in behalf of these unratified treaties both among the people and in the halls of legislation had a powerful enlightening influence, and contributed much to the success of the Hague Conference.

After the Hague Convention went into effect and the Permanent Court of Arbitration was established, new efforts began to be put forth for special treaties of obligatory arbitration, this time stipulating reference of controversies to the newly established tribunal. These efforts have been remarkably successful, though not yet completely so. No less than fifty-one treaties of this type were signed before the opening of the second Hague Conference on June 15, 1907, and since the second Hague Conference the number has increased to about eighty, twenty-four of which were negotiated by Secretary Root between January, 1908, and February, 1909, when he retired from the State Department. These treaties have all been ratified by the

Senate, and most of them already proclaimed by the President. In addition to the seventy-seven treaties given in the list,[1] fifteen others, all of them, except the Mexico-Persian treaty, between South American countries and Spain and South American countries themselves, must be added, carrying the whole number to above ninety. These fifteen treaties were signed before October 14, 1903, when the Franco-British treaty was announced.

These special treaties of obligatory arbitration, with three or four exceptions, lack much of being ideal, as they run for but five years, and provide only for the reference to the Hague Court of questions of a judicial order and those regarding the interpretation of treaties. With the exception of the treaties between Denmark on the one hand and the Netherlands, Italy and Portugal on the other, which have no limitations either in regard to time or to classes of cases, they all exclude from their operation questions which affect the " vital interests " and the " honor " of the signatories, — very vague and indefinite conceptions. The Swedish-Norwegian treaty does, however, stipulate that if a dispute shall be thought to involve vital interests or honor, this preliminary question shall first be referred to the Hague Court for determination. But in spite of their

---

[1] See pages 119–121.

limitations, these treaties mark a great step forward. The simple fact that great and mighty nations have become willing to pledge themselves in advance to submit important classes of disputes to a disinterested tribunal, the creation of their own joint action, speaks more eloquently than any words can possibly do of the growing international respect for law, of the more rational and humane attitude which the nations in general now bear toward one another, an attitude before which war with its unspeakable cruelties and its conspicuous failures of justice cannot long survive.

The second Peace Conference at The Hague during the summer of 1907 greatly advanced the cause of arbitration toward its final triumph. It enlarged and strengthened the Convention for the Pacific Settlement of International Disputes, adopted at the Conference of 1899, under which the Court of Arbitration was established. It provided that in case either of the governments parties to a dispute shall decline to arbitrate when requested to do so, the other party may go directly to the Bureau of the Hague Court and publicly ask for the arbitration of the controversy, a provision which when carried out will make it extremely improbable that any nation will, in face of the public opinion of the world, refuse to submit to arbitration any except the most extreme case.

The Conference, again, drafted a convention which prohibits the use of force for the collection of contractual debts from debtor nations until arbitration has first been tried or refused. This convention virtually brings all questions of money indemnity under the principle of obligatory arbitration, as it is in the highest degree improbable that any debtor nation would ever refuse to arbitrate a question of this kind.

The article in the Convention for the Pacific Settlement of International Disputes which provides for the creation of Commissions of Inquiry in cases where the dispute is chiefly concerned with facts, is properly to be classed with the arbitration provisions, for, as was proved in the Dogger Bank incident, such commissions, while not formally so, will in practice prove to be truly arbitration boards. The second Hague Conference strengthened the provisions for the creation of such commissions of inquiry so as to make them more efficient.

But the enormous progress which arbitration has made in the public opinion of the world is illustrated in nothing better than in the action of the second Hague Conference on the subject of obligatory arbitration. The principle of obligatory arbitration was approved by the Conference without a dissenting vote. Unanimous also was the declaration that certain differences, particularly those having to do

with the interpretation of treaties, are susceptible of
being submitted to obligatory arbitration without
any restriction. The form of treaty of obligatory
arbitration which was proposed by the United States
delegation to the Conference, which stipulated that
certain classes of controversies should go spontaneously to the Hague Court, received the votes of
thirty-five of the forty-four delegations, and only
five voted against it, four abstaining from voting.
The vote in favor of the proposition was therefore,
by nations, seven to one (by the populations represented, it was even greater), and but for the rule of
unanimity which governed the action of the Conference, we should to-day have a general treaty of
obligatory arbitration covering all questions of a
judicial order and those arising in the interpretation
of treaties binding the great body of the nations
together. The delegations which voted against the
American proposition at The Hague were those of
Germany, Austria, Greece, Roumania and Turkey.
But Germany, which led this opposition, was careful to explain that she was not opposed to obligatory
arbitration in principle, but was not ready to sign an
agreement of this kind with all the powers, the more
backward as well as the more advanced.

It appears from these facts that arbitration has
already essentially triumphed, and there is little
doubt that by the end of the third Hague Conference

the cause will have been completely won. Indeed, the nations are just on the point of going beyond arbitration, in the ordinary sense of that word. The second Hague Conference cast its vote unanimously for the creation of a regular international court of justice with judges always in service and holding regular sessions. It failed to find a method of appointing the judges which would be satisfactory alike to the great and the small powers, but this difficulty will undoubtedly be surmounted in a comparatively short time. The world, therefore, seems about to enter upon the era of judicial organization which will take international controversies out of the domain of violence and national conceit and passion and bring them under the dominion of law and reason. This is the great end toward which the arbitration movement has been tending, and which it is certain soon to reach under the pressure of the many forces which are now with ever-increasing energy and directness operating for its consummation.

CHRONOLOGICAL LIST OF ARBITRATION TREATIES WITH
DATES OF SIGNATURE

France and Great Britain	14 October, 1903
France and Italy	23 December
Great Britain and Italy	1 February, 1904
Denmark and the Netherlands	12 February
Spain and France	26 February
Spain and Great Britain	27 February

France and the Netherlands	6 April, 1904
Spain and Portugal	31 May
France and Norway	9 July
France and Sweden	9 July
Germany and Great Britain	12 July
Great Britain and Norway	11 August
Great Britain and Sweden	11 August
The Netherlands and Portugal	1 October
Belgium and Russia	30 October
Belgium and Switzerland	15 November
Great Britain and Portugal	16 November
Great Britain and Switzerland	16 November
Italy and Switzerland	16 November
Norway and Russia	26 November
Russia and Sweden	26 November
Belgium and Norway	30 November
Belgium and Sweden	30 November
Austria-Hungary and Switzerland	3 December
France and Switzerland	14 December
Sweden and Switzerland	17 December
Norway and Switzerland	17 December
Austria-Hungary and Great Britain	11 January, 1905
Belgium and Spain	23 January
Spain and Norway	23 January
Spain and Sweden	23 January
Great Britain and the Netherlands	15 February
Denmark and Russia	16 February
Italy and Peru	18 April
Belgium and Greece	19 April
Belgium and Denmark	26 April
Spain and Honduras	5 May
Portugal and Norway	6 May
Portugal and Sweden	6 May
Italy and Portugal	11 May
Belgium and Roumania	27 May
Portugal and Switzerland	18 August
Argentina and Brazil	7 September

Denmark and France	15 September, 1905
Denmark and Great Britain	25 October
Norway and Sweden	26 October
Denmark and Spain	1 December
Denmark and Italy	16 December
Austria-Hungary and Portugal	13 February, 1906
Denmark and Portugal	20 March, 1907
Spain and Switzerland	14 May
Italy and Mexico	16 October
Argentina and Italy	16 October
United States and France	10 February, 1908
United States and Switzerland	29 February
United States and Italy	8 March
United States and Mexico	24 March
United States and Great Britain	4 April
United States and Norway	4 April
United States and Portugal	6 April
United States and Spain	20 April
United States and the Netherlands	2 May
United States and Sweden	2 May
United States and Japan	5 May
United States and Denmark	18 May
United States and China	8 October
United States and Peru	5 December
United States and Salvador	21 December
United States and Argentina	23 December
Great Britain and Colombia	30 December
United States and Bolivia	7 January, 1909
United States and Ecuador	7 January
United States and Haiti	7 January
United States and Uruguay,	9 January
United States and Chile	13 January
United States and Costa Rica	13 January
United States and Austria-Hungary	15 January
United States and Brazil	23 January

THE TWO HAGUE CONFERENCES
AND THEIR RESULTS[1]

THE CONFERENCE OF 1899

IN view of the approach of the second Hague Conference, it is important to recall the meeting and work of the first, seven years ago, and to note the results which have followed it, and the immense progress which, through its influence and for other reasons, the cause of international peace has since made. In this way some proper estimate may be formed of what may reasonably be expected of the second Conference, about which a good deal of skepticism is already being manifested by some.

The famous Rescript of the Czar of Russia, suggesting the Conference, was handed to the diplomatic representatives of the other governments at St. Petersburg on the 24th of August, 1898. Notwithstanding the surprise which followed and the general doubt as to the possibility of accomplishing anything, all of the governments of Europe, twenty in number, four from Asia, and the United States and Mexico in America, approved of the Czar's

---

[1] From the *Advocate of Peace*, April, 1906.

proposal and decided to send delegates. A second
Rescript was consequently sent out by the Russian
government on the 11th of the following January,
outlining in some measure the subjects to be discussed. The actual assembling of the Conference
was entrusted to the government of the Netherlands, Queen Wilhelmina and her Minister, under
whose auspices it was held.

Several influences seem to have operated upon the
Czar to induce him to call the Conference. The
chief of these were the great work of John de Bloch
on "The Future of War," which he had carefully
studied and which had deeply impressed him; the
report of the special commissioner whom he had sent
in 1896 to Budapest to attend the Interparliamentary Conference and to inform him as to its
work and purposes; and, thirdly, the general condition of the masses of the European people, especially those of his own empire, brought on by the
excessive exactions of the great armaments. Added
to these were the dying charge of his father, who
had laid upon him the peace of the world as his
special mission, and the general progress of the
arbitration and peace movement, on which he was
well informed, and in which some eminent Rus-
sians, like Professor de Martens, had taken a conspicuous practical part.

The Conference met on the 18th of May, 1899,

and continued in session till the 29th of July. Baron
de Staal, head of the Russian delegation, was chosen
president. There were one hundred members of the
Conference, besides secretaries and other attendants.
The first week was devoted principally to organization, to official calls and receptions, to receiving
memorials, telegrams, cablegrams, letters and personal representations, the great number of which
from all parts of the civilized world revealed the
enormous amount of public interest and expectation
which the assembling of the Conference had awakened. The subjects on the program were assigned
to three large committees, one on armaments, one
on the rules and customs of war, and the third on
arbitration, and so forth. These committees did the
work, the Conference itself not meeting, after the
completion of its organization, except to act on
the committee reports at the end.

Though the Conference had been called primarily
to consider how relief might be secured from the
burdens of the great armaments, the committee to
whom this matter was entrusted soon found that
the Russian proposals on this subject awakened too
much opposition to allow anything positive to be
done. It limited itself therefore to the proposal of a
resolution declaring the great desirability of the
finding of relief from the heavy military burdens
resting upon the peoples. This resolution was

adopted by the Conference. The committee on the laws of war drafted and the Conference adopted a convention giving a body of improved rules for the conduct of " civilized " war on land, and one for the extension of the Red Cross to naval warfare. These conventions have since been approved by most of the states represented in the Conference. Three declarations were also made, one prohibiting for five years the throwing of projectiles and explosives from balloons, another prohibiting the use of projectiles designed to diffuse asphyxiating gases, and a third prohibiting the use of bullets which expand or flatten easily in the human body. Resolutions were adopted expressing the wish that an early conference should meet to revise the Geneva Red Cross Convention, that the rights and duties of neutrals should be dealt with by another conference, that the governments should attempt to arrive at an agreement concerning the adoption of new types and calibres of muskets and marine artillery, that they should study the possibility of an agreement for the limitation of armaments and war budgets, and that the subject of the immunity of private property at sea in war time, and that of the bombardment of forts, cities, and the like, should be referred for examination to another conference.

The great constructive work of the Conference was of course the Convention for the Pacific Settle-

ment of International Controversies, in sixty-one
articles. In this measure there was profound and
nearly universal interest, for the Conference soon
discovered that on this subject it had the mandate
of the civilized world. No less than five of the
delegations presented plans for a general system of
arbitration, including a permanent tribunal. The
only delegation that created any obstacle was that
from Germany, and this difficulty was quickly
got over as the result of a deputation sent to
Berlin. The Convention was threefold: it provided
for special mediation by neutral powers, for international commissions of inquiry in cases where disputes chiefly concerned facts, and for the creation
of a Permanent International Court of Arbitration.

The final act of the Conference, including the
three conventions, the declarations, the resolutions,
the wishes and a most significant preamble in which
the governments declared that they were " ani-
mated by a strong desire to concert for the maintenance of the general peace," and " resolved to
promote by their best efforts the friendly settlement
of international disputes," was signed on the 29th
of July.

The ratification of this Convention by the signatory powers went on gradually for nearly two years,
until, by April, 1901, some sixteen of them had
officially approved it and appointed their members

of the Permanent International Court. The Court was then, by the Netherlands Minister of Foreign Affairs, declared to be organized and ready for work. In all, twenty-two of the signatory powers have finally ratified the treaty, and the Court as at present constituted consists of seventy-two members, four being the maximum number allowed to be named by one government. The Permanent Bureau of the Court is at The Hague, and is under the care of an Administrative Council consisting of the Ministers from other countries accredited to the Netherlands, some thirty or more in number. The noble gift of $1,500,000 by Mr. Carnegie has made possible a worthy building for the Court. The Netherlands government has selected and purchased at The Hague a site for this building, the " Palace of Peace," and architects of many countries are now competing for the prize offered for the best plans for the structure. It is expected that the corner-stone of the building will be laid within a year.

After the Court was declared open, certain of the European powers seem for a time to have studiously ignored it. It was happily brought into operation by the treaty concluded in May, 1902, between the governments of the United States and Mexico for the submission to its jurisdiction of the Pious Fund controversy. The case was heard in September and October of that year and quickly decided, at small cost. The court which heard the case consisted of five judges chosen from the body of seventy-two, each nation naming two, and these four choosing the fifth. Since then three further cases have been adjudicated by the Court in a similar way, the Venezuela preferential question, to which eleven nations were parties, the Japanese house-tax controversy between Japan on one side and Great Britain, France and Germany on the other, and the dispute between Great Britain and France as to their respective rights under treaty stipulations with the Sultan of Muscat.

It will thus be seen that most of the first-class powers of the world have been before the Court, which has thus been given the most effective sort of practical recognition.

Another feature of the Hague Convention, the provision for international commissions of inquiry, was brought into operation in the case of the North Sea incident between Great Britain and Russia, and proved itself to be a most admirable instrument for the purpose for which it was devised, the determination of the controverted facts lying at the basis of disputes. Strong efforts were made several times during the course of the Russo-Japanese War to secure the application of the provision of the Hague Treaty for special mediation by the signatory powers, but unfortunately without result.

The action of President Roosevelt in bringing the belligerents together in conference with a view to ending the war was greatly facilitated by the provision of the Convention that a tender of good offices by a neutral should not be considered an unfriendly act. It is very doubtful if his efforts would have been successful, or even made, but for this clause of the Convention.

This simple recital makes it clear that the results of the first Hague Conference have been most important and lasting, beyond all that could have been expected in so short a time. We have been given through it the auspicious beginnings of a recognized international judicial order, which only needs patient employment and fuller development to put an end to the international chaos and violence which have hitherto so largely prevailed, and bring the nations in their relations to one another up to something like the standard of settled peace and pacific adjustment of differences which obtain among their citizens within their borders.

The establishment and successful early work of the International Court have already removed much of the doubt which had been felt by many as to the practicability of such an institution. Its decisions, though in one instance at least severely criticised, have been in general accepted as impartial and satisfying the ends of justice and honor. The way has thus been cleared for the early perfecting of the world's judicial system, and enthusiasm for the great cause of which the Court is the largest and most assuring public expression has been vastly widened and deepened. The treaties of obligatory arbitration, of which no less than forty have been concluded within the short space of two and a half years, stipulating reference of certain classes of controversies to the Court's jurisdiction, are the direct fruit of the Hague Conference and its far-reaching work. They have greatly strengthened the prestige of the Court with the governments and deepened the confidence of the general public in it.

We may feel assured, therefore, that even if the Hague Tribunal should remain just as it now is, without further development, it would in time prove, with the aid of the other provisions of the Convention, a fairly adequate means for upholding justice and settled peace among the nations. But the situation that has been brought about by the Conference of 1899 points just as surely to greater triumphs at the approaching Hague gathering. The nature of these we have frequently pointed out, and shall have occasion to set forth more fully hereafter, when the date of the Conference has been finally fixed.

THE CONFERENCE OF 1907 [1]

The second Hague Conference, called originally by President Roosevelt, but actually assembled by the Czar of Russia, met on the 15th of June, 1907, and continued in session till the 18th of October. All of the independent nations of the world except Costa Rica, Honduras, Abyssinia and Liberia were represented in it, the former two of these having been invited to send delegates. There were, including attachés and secretaries, two hundred and forty-four members of the Conference. Of these, twelve were ambassadors, thirty ministers plenipotentiary, fifteen members of the present Hague Court, and about a dozen had been members of the first Hague Conference. The Conference will always be notable as the first general representative assembly of the world.

Both during the latter part of the Conference and since its close there has been much unfavorable criticism of it. It has even been pronounced a failure and a farce. This pessimistic feeling, however, does not seem to me to be well founded, as careful analysis of the results of the Conference will clearly show.

The only sense in which the second Hague Conference can be considered a failure is that it did

---

[1] From the *Advocate of Peace*, February, 1908.

not accomplish all that the most advanced advocates
of international peace thought that it ought to accomplish. No attention need be paid to the utterances of the small class of critics who, because of
their attachment to the present military and naval
order of things, really wished the Conference to fail.
If the Conference had reached agreements for
the immediate limitation and early reduction of
armaments, for the conclusion of a general treaty of
obligatory arbitration providing for the reference
of all international controversies to arbitration, if
it had formally established a permanent International Court of Justice with judges always in service
and holding regular sessions of the Court, if it had
made all unoffending private property at sea exempt
from capture in war time, and had provided that war
should never be resorted to until the question in dispute had been examined by an impartial International Commission of Inquiry — if it had done all
these things, in addition to what it actually accomplished, the most sanguine peace idealist would not
have charged it with failure. The large feeling of
disappointment that the Conference did no more
than it did is a most hopeful omen. It means that
the public sentiment of the world, at least the most
intelligent part of it, is already considerably farther
advanced in the demand for general and permanent
peace than the governments are yet ready to go.

It would be unfortunate for the cause if this were not so. This advanced state of public opinion assures us that the movement is hereafter to have a regular and certain growth until the great ideals for which the peace movement stands are ultimately essentially realized.

One's estimate of the accomplishments of the Conference will depend very largely on one's point of view. If it be viewed as a single gathering with a definite program, without relation to the past or to the future, it may well be regarded, in considerable measure, a failure. Unfortunately, this is the point of view from which many have regarded it. If, on the contrary, it be looked at as the outcome of the long processes of civilization, especially of the peace and arbitration propaganda of the last hundred years, and as the beginning of a series of world assemblies to meet periodically hereafter for deliberation upon the great coming problems of the nations, then it seems to me that the Conference must be regarded as a conspicuous and memorable success; and this is the only sane point of view from which to regard it.

In the way of positive accomplishments the Conference has made a much greater record than is generally supposed. I am sure that all well-informed persons would so regard it, if the conventions actually reached were fully known and understood. Unfortunately, they have come to the public knowledge only in a scrappy and imperfect way. Some of the most important of them were scarcely alluded to in the press reports. This imperfect knowledge was probably inevitable, as the text of the conventions could not be published in full until they had been reported by the Conference to the governments at home. However, our knowledge is now complete enough to enable us to make up a fair judgment as to the results of the deliberations.

Of the fourteen conventions adopted, the most important is that for the Pacific Settlement of International Controversies, in ninety-seven articles. The basis of this is the convention adopted by the first Hague Conference, under the provisions of which the permanent Court of Arbitration was set up. The recent Conference revised and considerably strengthened the old convention, and issued it as an entirely new document. We have in this document the great work of the first Hague Conference reaffirmed, with a number of important improvements. The chief of these improvements are those which relate to the procedure of the Hague Court, to the use of International Commissions of Inquiry in the case of controversies where the dispute chiefly concerns facts, and the provision in Article 48, that in case of a conflict between two powers either of them, if the other hesitates or is disinclined to refer

the matter to the Hague Court, may go directly to
the Bureau of the Court and declare that it desires
to have the difference arbitrated. In the convention
adopted in 1899 the two powers had to agree before
the Court could be approached. This new provision
makes it possible for one of the powers to make an
offer of arbitration through the Court before the
public opinion of the world. The American Delegation, who introduced this provision, believed that
it would be morally impossible for any nation to refuse to arbitrate a dispute when the offer was thus
openly made before the world. The moral power
of the Hague Court, as it now exists, is therefore
very greatly increased through this new provision.

The next most important accomplishment is the
convention prepared by General Horace Porter,
after the extended discussions of the Drago Doctrine,
prohibiting the employment of force in the recovery
of contractual debts until arbitration to determine
the justice of the claim has been resorted to or refused by the debtor country. This convention practically extends the principle of obligatory arbitration
to the entire class of questions of monetary claims.
If ratified and put into force, there is little doubt
that this agreement will put an end hereafter to the
disgraceful conduct of a number of nations in attempting to force, by arms, the settlement of debts
due by governments to certain of their citizens,

without previous inquiry into the justice of the claims.

The third most important convention is that prohibiting the bombardment by naval forces of unfortified cities and ports in time of war; the fourth, that for the establishment of an International Prize Court. This latter has been considered by many, including some of the foremost delegates at The Hague, as the greatest result of the Conference. This convention sets up in time of war an international tribunal for the consideration of captures made during hostilities, to take the place of, or to serve as a court of appeal from the decisions of, the national Prize Courts which have heretofore been employed. Though this agreement is a regulation of war, it greatly extends the principle of international coöperation, and the general effect of it will doubtless be to diminish the chances of war, as well as to limit its lawlessness when once under way. The convention which declares that hereafter all fishing fleets over the whole surface of the oceans shall be inviolable is also a most important one, as it removes one of the great industries of the world from the perils of violence. Equally important is that which provides for the inviolability of the international mail service. Not less important is the convention declaring the territory of neutrals inviolable. This is only an embodiment in the form of international law of what has in most cases in recent years been the practice of the leading powers.

The agreement which extends the principles of the Geneva Red Cross Convention of 1864 to maritime warfare crystallizes into public international law what has already come to be substantially the practice of the leading maritime powers. This convention widens the application of the spirit of mercy and kindness, the spirit which is behind every phase of the peace movement, and will ultimately make war itself impossible. The conventions in regard to the placing of submarine mines, the prohibition of the throwing of projectiles and explosives from balloons, the restriction of the right of capture in maritime war, the one requiring a declaration of war before the opening of hostilities, and the others dealing with the laws and customs of war on land, the rights and duties of neutral powers in both land and maritime war, the transformation of merchantmen into warships, are all in the direction of the limitation and restriction of war. In these conventions the whole body of the nations of the world have for the first time in history jointly laid the hand of restriction heavily upon war. If these conventions shall be ratified by the powers, and even reasonably well carried out, war will hereafter be much more difficult than in the past, and to this extent will be much less likely to occur.

The greatest work of the Conference was that done outside of what has been incorporated into these formal conventions. On the subject of limitation of armaments, on which such deep and widespread interest was felt in all countries, no practical agreement was reached. But the subject was much discussed in private at The Hague, and the urgency of the problem has been made much clearer through the resolution unanimously adopted declaring that the study of the question by the governments with a view to some early practical solution is " highly desirable " — these were the words of the resolution — in the interests of the people of the world.

The same is true of the principle, so long advocated by our government, of the inviolability of all unoffending private property at sea in time of war. The greatest speech delivered in the Conference was made on this subject by Mr. Choate, and the principle received the hearty support of at least thirty-seven or thirty-eight of the powers. The measure was defeated by the opposition of the British government. But for this opposition, which is difficult to account for in a government professing to be highly civilized, the principle would now be a recognized part of public international law, as it certainly will be in a few years.

No agreement was reached by the Conference on the subject of a general treaty of obligatory arbitration, even of limited scope. But the principle of such a treaty was approved by more than three-fourths of the governments represented. Germany, which led the opposition, did not oppose the principle of obligatory arbitration, but felt that she could not at the present time enter into such an agreement with some of the less civilized powers. Obligatory arbitration has therefore been advanced by the Conference a long way toward final universal adoption.

In the matter of a permanent International Court of Justice presented and urged so strongly by the American Delegation, the Conference reached practical, if not altogether formal, agreement. The principle of such a court was adopted unanimously; this is most remarkable, as it was the first time that the proposition had been taken up and seriously discussed in a general international conference. The only failure was in reaching an agreement as to the method of selecting the judges. It is understood that this problem will be taken up by the governments themselves. Dr. James Brown Scott, Solicitor of our State Department, who was the American technical international law expert at the Conference and drafted the plan for this Court, has publicly declared that the Conference has actually settled this matter, and that we shall have this great Supreme Court of the World as the result of the Conference.

On one other subject also the Conference rendered possibly the greatest of all its services. It declared unanimously in favor of periodic Hague conferences hereafter, and set the date for the meeting of the next conference, about seven years hence. It also provided that a special commission appointed by the governments shall be created some two years in advance to study and prepare the program of the third Hague Conference. The recent Conference has therefore not only laid the foundations for a periodic Congress or Parliament of the Nations, which has been advocated by all the great international men of the past century, indeed of the past three centuries, but by its provision for the third Conference has actually inaugurated the greatest possible institution which can be conceived in the interests of the order and peace of the world.

It would not be far from the truth if one should say that the greatest and most far-reaching result of the Conference was the Conference itself. That all, or practically all, of the nations of the world should meet in a general assembly and continue in session four months discussing with perfect frankness, and yet with absolute fairness and friendliness, the great problems in which they are all so deeply interested, is a fact of marvellous significance. If the Conference had done nothing else, it would have been worth a thousand times all that it cost. The difficulties of such a meeting were much greater than many suppose. It would not have been surprising if the historic dislikes and prejudices, the differences of race, language and judicial methods, the force of local interests and ambitions, had made the gathering short-lived and valueless. But these were all overcome. The Conference lasted much longer than was expected, and the spirit of conciliation and concord grew in depth and strength to the very last. The experiment of a world assembly has been tried and proved a remarkable success. Other conferences will follow, and the world will no longer move in sections and halves, as heretofore, but as one united world; and the final, and we may hope not very remote, outcome will be the universal and perpetual peace which the great leaders of civilization and progress have so long seen coming.

THE CASE FOR LIMITATION OF ARMAMENTS [1]

THE question of limitation and even of gradual reduction of armaments must be carefully differentiated from that of disarmament, complete and thorough-going. The demand for limitation of armaments put forward by the leaders of the peace movement is often unfairly assumed to be a demand for total disarmament. The most advanced pacifists, in whatever nation they may be found, and however radical may be their views theoretically as to the duty of the nations to disarm and live together in permanent peace under the dominion of love and law, are not at the present time urging disarmament as a practical measure. They know very well that before the happy time shall come when nations will " beat their swords into plowshares and their spears into pruning hooks " in any general way, a very wide educational work for the removal of false conceptions and old prejudices must be done, and the process of rapprochement among the nations, now so happily taking place, must be carried much

[1] *American Journal of International Law*, October, 1908, and *Advocate of Peace*, December, 1908. By permission.

farther than it has yet gone. The practical thing which they are demanding — and, as they think, on the best of grounds — is the immediate arrest of the present feverish rivalry in armaments and of the attending rapid increase in the already colossal army and navy budgets. This step they hold to be not only perfectly reasonable and practicable under the present conditions of the nations in their relations one to another, but also imperatively demanded in the interests of justice and the common welfare of the populations on whom the burden of keeping up the exhausting rivalry falls with such peculiar oppressiveness. Only the salient features of the argument, or group of arguments, by which this demand of the pacifists is supported, can be developed in a single article.

GREAT PREPARATIONS FOR WAR OUT OF HARMONY WITH OUR CIVILIZATION

The first and most impressive contention of the friends of peace of this way of thinking is that civilization is now so far advanced that not only is war itself out of date, but the colossal preparations for war, which meet the view in whatever direction one turns, are thoroughly out of harmony with the spirit, the social habits, the intellectual attainment, and the philanthropic institutions of the age. When one puts this general character of our civilization over against the colossal armaments of the time and looks at them with clear eye, the judgment pronounced is very much like that made when one looks at black and white; their total unlikeness is seen without any argument. Private war, which for many generations ravaged Europe, has disappeared. The duel remains in but few civilized countries, and where it is still tolerated it is for the most part a farce. Personal fights with fist or club are to-day nearly unknown, except among thugs and drunken brawlers, who constitute a very small portion of any ordinary community, and are easily taken care of by a moderate police force. The carrying of deadly weapons openly is no longer in vogue. The possession of concealed weapons about the person is not only illegal in most countries, but is so generally held to be disreputable that no gentleman cares to have it known that his hip pocket is the receptacle of a revolver.

Parallel with this crowding of violence and the implements of brutality into the background goes a noteworthy prevalence of social confidence and trust, rising in innumerable cases, over wide areas, into genuine sympathy, friendship, and much mutual service. Neighbor trusts neighbor. The man on this side of the street is not suspicious of the man on that side. The different sides of cities no longer look upon each other as natural enemies, to be hated and maltreated. Mountains and rivers do not now divide peoples into mutually exclusive and malevolent communities. Indeed mountains, rivers and seas may be said no longer to exist, to such an extent have modern means of communication brought all parts of the world into direct communication with all other parts. The unity of the world, on the material side, is no longer a dream; it is an accomplished fact. Solidarity of thought and feeling, of interest and purpose, prevails within the national boundaries over great areas of territory. Philanthropies innumerable, which look after the needy and helpless, have the sympathy and support of the whole people, and these philanthropies have already been, to a striking extent, internationalized. Educational and industrial enterprises, scientific, social, sanitary and many other types of endeavors, both individual and collective, are marked characteristics both of national and international life. Peoples within the national borders settle their disputes, where they have any, either by direct friendly negotiation, by the arbitration of friends, or through the courts of law and equity. We have, indeed, within most of the nations within which peoples of different races and languages are compacted into nationalities largely homogeneous, reached an era of practically universal and perpetual peace. Civil war has virtually disappeared. Men and communities live together, if not

without friction and misunderstanding, at least
without those outbursts of passion and violence
which only a few generations ago prevailed in all
countries, and expressed themselves in bloody and
ruinous wars.

It seems utterly incongruous in such an advanced
state of civilization in respect of individuals and
separate states, where reason and common sense so
largely prevail and the use of brute force is being
reduced in an ever-increasing degree, that the nations in their corporate capacities should hold war in
the highest honor, should keep themselves in a
chronic state of feverish preparation for it, and
should be increasing and multiplying their military
and naval establishments, especially the latter, with a
rapidity and at a cost never before even dreamed of.
It is difficult to conceive of folly and absurdity carried to a higher pitch than this. The fact that it has
always been so can no longer be made an excuse for
its continuance. Bad habits in nations are even less
excusable than in individuals. There is but one way
in which the states which constitute the so-called
family of nations can deliver themselves from the
guilt and burden of this folly, and that is by taking
steps at once to get together and solemnly agree that
the present competitive arming shall stop short and
go no further. No international act will be found
easier than this the moment the governments deter-

mine to undertake it with seriousness and with sincerity. There are many evidences which go to show that many of the governments themselves are already taking this view of the situation, though a few of them appeared at the last Hague Conference to have formed no real conception of the absurd nature of the situation.

A HUNDRED YEARS OF UNIFORMLY SUCCESSFUL ARBITRATION

In the development of arbitration during the past century, and in the holding and results of the two Hague Conferences, an equally weighty and even more immediately practical reason for arrest of armaments is found. It is generally conceded that reduction of armaments and ultimate disarmament, with the exception possibly of a small international police force, and such limited national armaments as may be necessary to insure protection against internal disorders, will follow naturally the establishment by the nations of an adequate substitute for war, on which every nation can rely for impartial consideration of its controversies and the rendering of just judgment. If this be true, as conceded, then what has already been accomplished in this direction, by agreement of substantially all the powers of the world, would seem to demand an immediate halt in the competitive increase of armaments, until such a

time as the attempt to create a world organization
with a High Court of Nations, which has so far
been successful beyond expectation, shall have
proved a failure. It is true that an international
High Court of Arbitral Justice is not yet in operation. This is true, however, formally rather than
really. Arbitration as a practical method of adjusting disputes between nations has been experimented
with for nearly a hundred years and with singularly
uniform success. Within this time at least two hundred and fifty international disputes, not to mention
as many more settlements which were of minor importance, have been successfully adjusted by this
means. In the case of all these settlements the
award, though in a few instances severely criticized,
has been loyally accepted by the defeated party.
Many of the disputes so adjusted have been of a
most delicate and difficult nature, in which both
national honor and vital interest have been conspicuously involved. Looking only to these *ad hoc*
arbitrations, it would seem that the powers of the
world, practically all of which have participated in
some of these settlements, had had experience
enough of the sufficiency and honorableness of this
method of settling differences to give them entire
confidence in it, and to induce them to be ready
hereafter to refer all controversies, of whatever
class, except those involving the national life, to

tribunals of arbitration. If a hundred years of such uniformly successful experience is not enough to satisfy them, how much, pray, will be needed to meet their demands?

Furthermore, within the past five years treaties of obligatory arbitration to the number of sixty have been concluded among all the important governments of the world. These treaties, with the exception of two or three, are, it is true, of a limited character. They stipulate the reference to the Hague Court or other tribunals of arbitration only of questions of a judicial order and those arising in the interpretation of treaties, categories which may well include all disputes of whatever nature that are likely ever again to arise among the states whose boundaries are in general now well fixed, and whose limits and integrity are almost universally recognized and respected. The full force of these arbitral agreements is scarcely realized even by the governments themselves. The French Foreign Office has recently published, in connection with a report on the proceedings of the last Hague Conference, a chart showing in a most graphic way the binding together of thirty-five of the capitals of the world by this network of treaties. The bond thus created constitutes a new bulwark against war, and a new and peculiarly strong ground for international confidence. Even in this fragmentary way, therefore,

the governments have found a substitute for war in
dealing with controversies, which is practically, if
not theoretically and formally, adequate to the
maintenance of both justice and honor in all cases
of disagreement among them.

ARBITRATION COURT A PRACTICALLY ADEQUATE
SUBSTITUTE FOR WAR

But the process here referred to has been carried
much further through the Hague Conferences of
1899 and 1907. In the first of these Conferences
twenty-six of the powers of the world, including all
those of the first rank, were represented. In the
latter practically all of the powers, great and small,
took part. It was, to all intents and purposes, a world
assembly, and it discussed all of the questions with
which it dealt in the spirit of a world assembly. It
carried on its deliberations in a way that demon-
strated once for all that a world congress or parliament is in every way practical, and that problems of
a universal order can be dealt with in such an assembly with fairness toward all, and with a delib-
erateness and considerateness which will prevent the
serious offending of the sensibilities of any country,
small or great, and which will insure justice to each
of the nations in a manner possible in no other way.
The unanimous vote of the Conference in favor of
periodic meetings at The Hague hereafter, and the

fixing of the date of the third Hague Conference some seven years hence, with a plan for adequate preparation of the program by an international commission, has practically settled the question of a periodic world assembly, which, it is now generally believed, will meet as regularly hereafter as the national parliaments, and, though advisory only in its character at first, will grow gradually into a parliament with ever-increasing legislative powers. For the purpose of this discussion, it need be only mentioned that the Conference revised and considerably improved the Convention for the Pacific Settlement of International Disputes drawn by the first Hague Conference, and sent it forth as a new treaty, this time with the signatures of representatives not of twenty-six powers, but of all the powers of the globe, with one or two unimportant exceptions. Under this Convention the Permanent Court of Arbitration, set up under the Convention of 1899, has become a real world court, to which all the nations are now parties, and to which every one of them may have recourse. There exists, therefore, in this arbitration court, though reference of disputes to it is still only voluntary, a substitute for war which in practice will prove itself to be entirely adequate to meet the ends of justice in any cases of differences likely ever to arise hereafter. But the Conference, as is well known, went further along this line. It voted unanimously for the establishment of a supreme world court of arbitral justice, with judges always in service and holding regular sessions, a court holding practically the same relation to the nations as the Supreme Court of the United States holds to the separate states of our Union. And if the Conference's recommendation to the governments in regard to finding a satisfactory method of selecting the judges is seriously and faithfully carried out, a supreme court of the nations will be in actual existence and thoroughly organized by the time the next Hague Conference assembles. In any event, the court will be organized and put into operation at no distant day, and in the meantime the present Hague Court of Arbitration will do substantially the same work, which will finally go to the High Court of Arbitral Justice.

This process of world organization and of the extension of arbitration and of arbitral justice in an organized way to the international sphere having gone as far as it has, it is difficult to understand how the governments can find any rational justification for the perpetual increase of their military and naval establishments on a scale and with a haste which would lead one naturally to suppose that no relations of friendship and coöperation existed among them, that they had never met in conference, that treaty relations were practically unknown to

them, and that they were still living in the anarchic
state of the barbarous ages. There is no such justification. The eminent success which arbitration has
attained and the advanced state of organization of
the institutions which the Hague Conferences are
creating require, if the analogy of the development
of law and order and the reduction of the use of
force within the nations has any value, that the
governments which are parties to the Hague Conventions — that is, the governments of the entire
world — should at once take steps to diminish their
reliance on and use of force in their relations one
to another. It might fairly be contended, from the
government point of view, that these institutions
have not yet been developed to a point of perfection
where anything like complete disarmament or any
very large reduction in the military and naval establishments should be immediately undertaken. But
it may, on the other hand, be contended with even
greater force that what the governments are doing
in the perpetual enlargement of these war establishments and the increasing burdens which are being
laid upon the people for their maintenance is entirely
out of harmony with what they are doing in binding themselves together in pacific treaty relations
and with the deliberate way in which they are entering into a universal and permanent organization
through the Conferences at The Hague. They ought

at once either to provide for the arrest of the growth of their great military and naval preparations, or to throw up the Hague Conferences, the Hague Conventions, the treaties of obligatory arbitration and the like. There is no other way in which the claim of sincerity and consistency can be maintained by them.

LIMITATION DEMANDED BY ECONOMIC CONSIDERATIONS

The ground most commonly urged in favor of an arrest of armaments is the immense and ever-increasing cost of maintaining and renewing them, especially of the new naval constructions which this rivalry necessitates. This argument for limitation, though not as fundamental as those given above, is the most striking and impressive one, especially to the common mind. In a memorial recently presented to the British Prime Minister, signed by one hundred and forty-four members of the House of Commons, urging an arrest of the military and naval expenditures of Great Britain, Mr. Asquith's attention was recalled to the fact, already noted by him, that in the last ten years the expenditure on the British army had advanced from eighteen millions to nearly thirty millions of pounds sterling, an increase of sixty-three per cent, while the cost of maintaining and increasing the navy for the same period had advanced from twenty-two to nearly thirty-two millions of pounds, or about forty-three per cent. This memorial, quoting from the government budget, also pointed out that the total cost of maintaining both army and navy had gone up in the ten years from forty millions to sixty-one millions of pounds, an aggregate increase of fifty-two per cent. It is a matter of common knowledge that in the last ten years the army and navy budgets of our own government have increased to an alarming degree, that of the navy being nearly three hundred per cent, and at the present time we are spending on the two services, including fortifications, no less than two hundred and twenty millions of dollars per year. The conditions of the other great powers are practically the same. The total cost of maintaining the armies and navies of the world at the present time aggregates, according to the speech of the British Prime Minister at the banquet given to the London Peace Congress on the 31st of July, this year, not much less than four hundred millions of pounds, or nearly two billions of dollars per year. At the lowest figure it is one and a half billions.

This reckoning takes no account of the fifteen hundred millions of dollars required each year to meet the interest on the huge debts of the national treasuries, which amount in the aggregate at the present time to no less than thirty-five thousand millions of dollars, nearly the whole of which is due to the wars of the last half century. These enormous burdens affect the welfare and happiness of the people in two ways. They add, first, directly to the tax burdens of the people of the nations. The expenditure of three hundred millions of dollars and more by Great Britain on the army and navy means a tax of not less than thirty-seven dollars annually per family, or over seven dollars per individual of the entire population. In our own case the military and naval burden of taxation rises to at least twelve dollars per family. This is no small item, considering the fact that the average income of the families of the nation is not over six hundred dollars per year each. If the present rivalry continues, the tax burden will increase in an even greater ratio, as the Dreadnaughts and other constructions now in contemplation will cost from two to four times as much as vessels of the same class have cost in the past. Nothing but the utmost necessity could possibly justify the governments in thus bleeding the people to keep up and increase these armaments; and the facts adduced above show conclusively that no such necessity exists. A very large amount of the money that goes in this way is therefore pure waste, and the people receive nothing in return for it except an imaginary protection, of which there is not the least need.

Again, this rivalry of armaments, besides taking so many men away from productive employments and thus reducing the national wealth, absorbs so much of the national revenue that many internal improvements, on which the welfare and prosperity of the people so much depends, have to go begging. Those who followed with any care the recent debates on the army and navy bills in Congress do not need to have this point amplified. Appropriations for river and harbor improvements, for public buildings, for the protection of forests, and for improvement of the land, are exceedingly difficult to obtain in amounts at all adequate to the needs, when two-thirds of the national revenue is consumed in preparation for imagined wars in the future or the payment of pensions and of interest on the war debts of the past. In this case also nothing but the utmost emergency could justify the withdrawal of these great sums of the public money from constructive enterprises in which all the people are interested, and the devoting of them to the instruments of war and destruction.

It will be remembered by the readers of this journal that all the governments take advantage of every possible occasion to declare to all the world that their armaments are not in any sense intended for aggressive purposes, but only for defence and for the preservation of general peace. If these professions are true, or even measurably true, they constitute one of the strongest possible reasons for an early agreement among them not to go any further in piling up these costly instruments of war. But while making, several times a year of late, these loud professions, each of the important powers involved in the present competitive arming by the course it is taking gives the lie to the other powers making the same claims of innocence as itself. How much does this lack of positive insult on the part of each nation to all the others? There is something extraordinarily ludicrous in this spectacle of the body of nations each claiming to be innocent of any evil intention against the others, and yet all of them racing away at warship building, army strengthening and fortification extension as if its sister powers were all unparalleled liars, in whom no particle of confidence was to be placed. This conduct seems hardly more rational than that hypothecated of certain alarmist military and naval men who, in the language of the late Lord Salisbury, would fortify the moon against an invasion from Mars. Has not the time come when the governments of the world should begin to proceed a little more like gentlemen in common society, who are accustomed to accept each other's word of honor as essentially true?

UNITED STATES MIGHT SAFELY CEASE TO INCREASE
HER NAVAL ARMAMENT

There remains to be considered only the question
whether any single nation, or pair of nations, or
small group of nations, can begin limitation of armaments without the coöperation and agreement of
all the others. The course taken by Chile and
Argentina in regard to the reduction of their forces
on both land and sea, after the settlement of their
long-standing boundary dispute, seems to be a sufficient answer to the second part of this question.
These two nations have not only been more prosperous since their partial disarmament, but no less safe
from attack by foreign powers, even their own
nearest neighbors. Nobody has any doubt that a
group of three or five of the powers of Western
Europe might at once, with perfect safety, without
any coöperation on the part of the other powers,
cease further to enlarge their armies and navies.
England, France and Germany, it would be universally conceded, could do this. France and England, possibly alone, but at any rate with the co-
operation of Italy, might with security take this
step, which there is no doubt would at once be followed with readiness and even great enthusiasm by
the other European powers.

It is not probable, however, that any European

government could be induced to see its way single-
handed to stop further increase of its military and
naval establishments. But the case is different with
the United States. The doubling of our standing
army and the still greater increase in the size of our
navy have been made on the theory that without
these preparations we should be in danger of early
attack on both our eastern and western coasts. But
this alleged reason for the course that the government has taken has been nothing but pure supposition. Not a single indisputable fact has been produced in its support. We have no foreign enemies.
In our entire history since the signing of the Constitution no nation has ever declared war against us
or threatened to attack us. We have ourselves begun all our foreign wars. No nation is threatening
to make war upon us at the present time for any
purpose whatever, least of all for the possession of
the Philippines. The suspicions which have been
mouthed about for the last ten years against Germany have every one of them proved to be ground-
less. No German settlement in Brazil, or any other
part of the Western world, would accept the sovereignty of the German Empire if freely permitted
to do so, for it was from the military burdens of
this empire that they fled across the sea. And there
is no evidence that the Imperial German Empire has
ever had any intention of attempting to impose its

sovereignty on any Western German colony. The recent craze over the supposed danger of war upon our western coast from Japan has been shown from innumerable sources to be not even "respectable nonsense," to use the language of a distinguished citizen of Japan. Guarded by three thousand miles of ocean on the east, and more than twice that on the west, and held in respect, so far as anybody knows, by every government on the face of the globe, as we are, it seems to many of us that even from the point of view of adequate national defence our government has already gone farther than any necessity requires, in the direction of arming itself against foes that do not exist, and, if they did, could not by any possibility do us serious harm, even if our army and navy were much less than they are at the present time.

COMMERCE NEEDS NO GREAT NAVY FOR ITS PROTECTION

The pretence that we need a steady increase of the navy to afford protection to our ever-expanding commerce has no real ground on which to stand. Piracy has gone from the seas. Commerce that behaves itself is free to go and come as it likes in any quarter of the globe, subject only to regulations to which the commerce-carrying vessels of all the

powers are alike amenable. Our foreign trade would
be just as safe and untrammelled if we had only a
half or a quarter of our present war fleet as it is now.
For commerce is an international thing, and the
real protection of it is not warships at all, but the
common interest of the nations and peoples in it,
and the general spirit of fairness, justice and confidence, of give and take, with which our civilization
is now so largely pervaded. It is this interest and
this spirit of trustful mutuality that have made the
great international trade of our day possible, that
have built it up to such immense proportions, that
sustain it and make it secure for us as well as for
other peoples. The fact is that the greater our
foreign trade the fewer the battleships we need to
protect it, for its increase unites us more and more
widely and intimately with all parts of the world, to
whose interest it is, as well as to ours, that our mer-
chant ships should go and come, enter ports and
leave them, with the fewest possible dangers and
obstacles. From this point of view a half dozen up-
to-date swift cruisers would be amply sufficient to
afford protection against violence to any of our ships
of commerce which might possibly still take place in
some out-of-the-way places remote from the general
influence of the civilized powers, though it would be
very difficult to point out where such out-of-the-
way places can any longer be found.

SUPPOSED NEW RÔLE IN THE WORLD DEMANDS NO ENLARGED NAVY

It hardly seems worth while to try to strengthen the case for limitation of armaments on the part of our own country by a criticism of the claim that we have for the first time, since the Spanish War, become a world power, and hence find ourselves under the necessity of making our navy steadily bigger in order to be able properly to play the new rôle that has come to us among the nations of the earth. This extraordinary bit of reasoning has been much used by the big-navy promoters, but the assumptions on which it is based are so vague and shadowy that a long preliminary discussion of them would be necessary before one could deal directly with the argument in any intelligent and comprehensive way. Have we for the first time become a world power? In what does a world power consist? What is the pretended new rôle that, as a world power, we are to be compelled to play? Must a new world power follow necessarily the militaristic and aggressive policies and methods of the old ones? Must world powers, old or new, forever stick to the crude and barbarous and brutal agencies and ideas which have marked the past? The examination of these and similar questions would lead the discussion too far afield. Suffice it to say that, what-

ever we may have become as a result of the Spanish
War, this transformation does not in the least
change our general continental situation between
the two great oceans, nor has ten years of possession
of our island dependencies furnished a single reason
for the development of our fleet beyond its present
proportions. The transformation does not modify in
any important respect the general character of the
advanced civilization in the midst of which we as a
people live, and from whose high moral obligations
and behests we cannot escape. It does not break
down — it rather increases — the growing unity
of the world, the complexity and strength of the
new world-society, with its widening coöperation
and sympathies, its growing trust and its sensibly
decreasing need of reliance on brute force. It has
strengthened rather than weakened the bulwark
which the colossal and ever-expanding commerce
of the world is erecting against war, and, still more,
against international enmity and explosions of passion. Nor again does the supposed transformation
that has come to us alter the results of the two
Hague Conferences. The laying of the foundations
of a regular world assembly and the setting up of
a durable guarantee of peace in the Permanent
International Court of Arbitration are accomplished
facts. The powerful bond of peace which has been
created among the nations by the conclusion of more

than sixty treaties of obligatory arbitration, to a dozen of which the United States is a party, is certainly not in the least weakened and endangered by the fact that our connection with the world has become wider and more intimate than it was a dozen years ago. Indeed, this new bond has been established since the date on which we were supposed to have become a " world power."

There is, then, in this direction not a shadow of ground for the further increase of our navy, unless the nation proposes to act the bully among the other nations and attempt to force its will upon unwilling powers and peoples regardless of justice and right, a supposition which even the most reckless defenders of a big and ever bigger navy would not care openly to champion. The whole weight of the argument for immediate limitation of our navy and army, drawn from the general international situation of the world and our own peculiar national position in particular, remains in all its force, rather strengthened than weakened by the larger and more prominent part which our country is now taking in the world's affairs.

LOGICAL THING FOR THE UNITED STATES TO DO

Under these conditions it seems that the logical thing for the United States government to do at the present time would be, without respect to what the other nations may or may not promise to do, to stop short in the increase of the army and of the navy, and let it be known to all the world that it will live as if it trusted the sister nations and was ready at any moment to unite with them in an agreement for general limitation of armaments. Such an example would almost certainly meet with an immediate and cordial response from the other nations on whom the burdens of the present conditions bear much more heavily than upon us.

But however this may be as to the United States or any other single nation, it seems perfectly clear, under all the conditions of the times, that it is the imperative duty of the governments, in their collective capacity, to reach an agreement which at a very early day will relieve them, one and all, from the burdens which have grown to be so great and exhausting, and which the peoples ought no longer to be called upon to bear. The nation that leads in inducing the powers of the world to take this step — and some nation ought at once to take the lead — will have won for itself a place of honor in the world's history than which it would be difficult to conceive a higher or a nobler.

LESSONS FROM THE HISTORY OF
THE PEACE MOVEMENT [1]

———

As I was entering these grounds and saw the big cannon guarding the approach to the stately and beautiful Capitol, I was reminded of the famous passage in the speech delivered by Victor Hugo at the opening of the Peace Congress at Paris, on August 22, 1849. He said:

" A day will come when the only battlefield will be the market opening to commerce and the mind opening to new ideas. A day will come when bullets and bombshells will be replaced by ballots, by the universal suffrage of nations, by the venerable arbitration of a great sovereign senate, which will be to Europe what the Parliament is to England, what the Diet is to Germany, what the Legislative Assembly is to France. A day will come when a cannon will be exhibited in public museums, just as an instrument of torture is now, and people will be amazed that such a thing could ever have been. A day will come when the two immense groups, the

———

[1] Address at the opening session of the New England Peace Congress, in the Capitol, Hartford, Conn., May 9, 1910.

United States of America and the United States of Europe, will be seen standing in the presence of each other, extending the hand of fellowship across the ocean, exchanging their produce, their commerce, their industry, their arts, their genius, clearing the earth, peopling the deserts, improving creation under the eye of the Creator, and uniting, for the good of all, these two irresistible and infinite powers, the fraternity of men and the power of God. Nor is it necessary that four hundred years should pass away for that day to come. We live in a rapid period, in the most impetuous current of events and ideas which has ever borne humanity along; and at the period in which we live a year suffices to do the work of a century."

The international peace movement has to-day reached a point of development and strength which makes it important to consider carefully the lessons which its history teaches, that we may avoid certain dangers to which its very successes and triumphs expose us at the present time.

Standing here in New England, where Worcester and Channing, Ladd and Burritt and Sumner and their co-laborers did their heroic work in the early days in organizing and developing the peace movement; here in Connecticut, where early organized peace effort grew with extraordinary rapidity and covered every county in the State by

1835; here in Hartford, where William Watson first published the *Advocate of Peace* in 1834, and where the American Peace Society pitched its tent for two years on its migration from New York to Boston; here where Horace Bushnell wrote his famous oration on " The Growth of Law," and prophesied that law would ultimately eliminate war from human society; here, not far from the place where Burritt, with his many tongues, and his Olive Leaf Mission, came near destroying the influence of the Tower of Babel — standing here, on holy ground, where the God of Peace long ago appeared unto men, one cannot refrain from asking what these pioneers of peace would say and how they would feel if they were with us at this hour.

That Worcester and Ladd and Burritt, the great New England trio of peace pioneers, would be surprised at what has been accomplished in a century is doubtful. They would almost certainly expect to find much more done. Their wonder would be that men have been so slow in accepting and putting into practice the international principles and policies which they advocated and believed to be perfectly reasonable and practicable.

But one may well imagine the intense interest and pleasure with which they would, nevertheless, listen to the remarkable story of the peace movement; the story of the growth of the peace societies

from three in 1815 to more than five hundred at
the present time, and their expansion from the narrow Atlantic seaboard to all quarters of the globe;
the successful application of arbitration, of which
they knew next to nothing in practice, to more than
two hundred and fifty important controversies in
less than a century, to some of which practically all
the important nations have been parties; the organization of peace congresses into a regular yearly
system, both national and international, and of special conferences like that at Lake Mohonk; the
creation of an international peace bureau, which
brings all the peace societies and congresses into
harmonious coöperation; the organization and most
effective work of the Interparliamentary Union of
statesmen for the past twenty-one years; the incep-
tion and remarkable development of the Pan-
American Union; the two Hague Conferences,
bringing together in friendly council and planning
all the nations of the world.

One can imagine William Ladd rising up and
standing with uncovered head as he listened to the
account of the setting up and the successful operation of the International Court of Arbitration at
The Hague; the conclusion of treaties of obligatory
arbitration to the number of nearly one hundred
between the nations, two and two, pledging reference of important classes of disputes to the Hague

Court; and the laying of the foundations of a world congress or parliament. Ladd and his co-workers would be deeply impressed with the enormous growth of public opinion everywhere in favor of a pacified and united world, and with the open and widespread demand on all sides that the system of armed suspicion and hostility, which has ruled the world from time immemorial, shall cease and the nations live henceforth as members of a common family. It is a marvellous story of effort and accomplishment which these fathers of peace would hear if they were with us to-day. There is almost nothing else like it in the whole history of humane progress.

The pioneers of the peace movement were men of remarkable insight, practical wisdom and unsurpassed courage. To tackle deliberately the war system, hoary with centuries and entrenched as it was in the laws, customs and habits of thought and feeling of men everywhere, with the expectation of overthrowing and finally destroying it, required a type of faith and heroism rarely found. What does their example and the fruit of their planting and training teach us?

They were first of all idealists, thorough-going idealists, as all men must be who move and lift the world. There are no really practical men except idealists. They saw clearly what the nations ought to be in their relations to one another, what the moral and social constitution of men and of societies of men demands as the true human state. They saw in the future an era without war; what the Germans call, in their splendid phrase, " *Die Krieglose Zeit.*" They proclaimed this ideal international condition as an obligation, the fulfillment of which, as fast as possible, was incumbent upon all men and nations. They further saw that the war system, as it had come down out of the past, was in its spirit and in its deeds and results totally at variance with this ideal, the greatest obstacle in the way of the attainment of the union of the nations and races; that it was indeed the very antithesis, the denial, the wreck of the normal, the predestined life of the world. They therefore arraigned it as both senseless and wicked, as the fruitful source of cruelty and injustice, as morally and economically ruinous. They saw that war was hell long before General Sherman was born, though they expressed it in somewhat different phraseology. Thus far their idealism carried them, both positively and negatively.

These early advocates of peace have been criticised as too sentimental; as dwelling too much on the horrors and cruelties, the savage ferocities of war. But they had to do it; otherwise their idealism would have been only half expressed. It is not certain but that a good deal of the same kind of treatment is still needed, unpleasant as it is to our modern minds, for the legend of the " righteousness " and the " glory " of war still lingers and deludes many souls.

But Dodge and Worcester and Ladd and Burritt and the rest of them were also thoroughly practical men. They did not naïvely assume that the warring world could be saved by merely proclaiming the ideal and condemning the actual condition of things. They did not go quite as far as Emerson, who said, in substance, that if you will only launch an idea it will do the rest itself. They saw that a large program of practical peace work was necessary, and this they inaugurated at once.

First of all, they started a campaign of education, by both tongue and pen, on the platform, in the pulpit and in the press, that public opinion might be won to the new views; and no more intelligent, vigorous and well-sustained campaign of reform has ever been carried on in the interest of any cause. This first campaign continued for more than forty years, till the Civil War began to throw its dark shadow over the land. Many of the foremost men of the country, then largely on the Atlantic Coast, engaged in it. Among them were Dodge, Worcester, Channing, Ladd, President Kirkland of Harvard, Whittier, Garrison, Burritt, Upham, Walker, May, Blanchard, the Tappans, Ballou, Henry C. Wright, Dr. Joseph Allen, Thomas S. Grimké, Charles

Sumner, Judge Jay and many others. These men left practically nothing new to be said on the subject. Their speeches and writings — the pamphlets of Dodge, Worcester's "Friend of Peace," the essays of Ladd, the addresses of Channing, the orations of Sumner, the essay of Emerson, the Manual of Upham, the papers and books of Judge Jay — remain to us as a great and permanent literature produced by that period, without which we modern workers would be poor indeed in our outfit. By 1840 the whole subject of a congress and court of nations had been presented and clearly and exhaustively expounded by them, along substantially the lines that the Hague Conferences have followed. No movement was ever better launched than the peace movement. It sprang almost full-fledged from the brains of these men, like Minerva from the head of Jupiter.

Along with, or rather as a part of, their campaign of educating public sentiment, these peace pioneers began at once to present and urge upon the governments of the world substitutes for war. Arbitration, with its concomitants, was almost as common in their mouths as it is in ours. Not only in their public addresses and in pamphlets and periodical publications did they urge this rational method of adjusting disputes, but also in memorials to our government. As early as 1816, the year after its establishment, the Massachusetts Peace Society sent a remarkable memorial to Washington, in which it urged the Congress to institute a deliberate inquiry with a view of ascertaining how the government might exert a pacific influence on human affairs; how it might help to infuse into international law a pacific spirit; how it might aid in diminishing the frequency, or in circumscribing the calamities, of war; how it might promote the general reference of controversies to an impartial umpire as the law of the Christian world, and might promote compacts " for the express purpose of reducing the enormous and ruinous extent of military establishments." That all sounds very recent and shows how far in advance of their time these men were. But they did not stop with these general recommendations. They urged the establishment of a world congress, or parliament, as the organ of the joint life of the nations. They advocated also the creation of a high court of nations for the judicial settlement of controversies. The first plan of the nineteenth century for an international tribunal was not worked out by the Hague Conferences, not by any Bar Association, not by the Interparliamentary Union, but by a group of New England men as early as 1840, of whom William Ladd was the chief.

The lines of work and influence thus inaugurated have been substantially followed ever since by the workers for peace, not only in this but in all countries. As far as circumstances have permitted, they have all been kept up and pushed at the same time. No one phase of the subject has, as a rule, been emphasized at the expense of others. The supreme importance of a widespread peace public opinion has been kept always in mind. Every effort possible, with the limited resources at hand, has been put forth to educate and concentrate public sentiment in behalf of the great ends sought. The advocates of peace have always, with Dr. Channing and Horace Bushnell, recognized the truth that public opinion rules the world. International justice, friendship and mutual service have always been contended for. The arbitration of all differences between nations has been urged and urged again, until this method of settlement has finally become the settled practice of the world, though not yet fully embodied in the law of nations. A permanent international court of justice as superior to and to take the place of temporary tribunals of arbitration has been urged from the beginning. A world assembly or parliament for the handling of the great interests common to the nations has been the object of a vast amount of thought and special effort. The irrationality and iniquity of great military and naval establishments, with their unceasing, increasing and ruinous burdens upon the people, have been faithfully and

unequivocally pointed out. Government consideration of all these problems and action upon them has
been urged, time and again, as the only possible way
in which the aims of the friends of peace can be at
last attained.

This, without going into further details, of which
there are many most interesting ones, has been the
program of the peace movement for a hundred
years. It is the necessary program still. There is
almost no phase of it which can yet be dropped.
Public opinion — much of it at any rate — is still
very benighted and reactionary about the movement. Many intelligent men, intelligent in other
respects, know nothing about the cause in which we
are laboring, and practically nothing about what
has been accomplished through the Hague Conferences.

Though the arbitration of disputes is now the
regular order, nearly all the governments persist in
refusing to agree to submit questions of " honor "
and " vital interests " to the Hague Court. In spite
of President Taft's most important utterance on this
subject recently, they seem likely to persist in this
refusal for some time yet. A general treaty of obligatory arbitration, to be signed by all the nations
and including all questions of difference between
governments, still remains to be concluded, though
great advance toward this accomplishment was

made at the second Hague Conference. The creation of a periodic congress or parliament of the nations is as yet only in its incipiency. What was accomplished in this direction at The Hague in 1907 leaves much yet to be done. Though the second Hague Conference voted its unanimous approval of the principle of an international high court of justice, the actual selection of the judges and the inauguration of the Court does not seem to be immediately in sight, notwithstanding the most important and hopeful efforts now being made by our Department of State. In the matter of arrest of the prevailing rivalry in armaments, especially in battleship building, the goal of our efforts seems still farther away. The old suspicions and jealousies and animosities lying behind these armaments die very hard, and before we can see any relief from the enormous burdens imposed upon the people by these great establishments, a great deal of thoroughgoing work in the transformation of national and racial feelings, prejudices and delusions must still be done.

It behooves the peace party of this country, indeed of all countries, to be true to all the great lines of this historic program. None of them can be neglected without crippling and retarding the whole movement. It behooves us also to be patient and steady, as well as active and energetic. There is no

short cut to peace. I sympathize with those of our
friends, some of them among the noblest supporters
of the cause, who, inspired by the marvellous advance already made, as well as by a deep sense of the
obligations of the hour in the presence of the appalling growth of war preparations, are impatient
to see a bold stroke made and the whole movement
brought to a sudden end, and war banished from the
earth " by one fell swoop." But nothing that has
been done toward the permanent peace of the world
has been accomplished by force and violence. Nothing can be done. It is too late now to resort, in the
interests of peace, to the very agency which brought
on war and has kept it in the world. No nation or
group of nations, led by no matter whom, can force
peace upon the world. Any such peace would go to
pieces almost as soon as made. " Force is no remedy," as John Bright was accustomed to say. The
nations, large and small alike, are vitally interested
in the matter. Whatever agency or method is
adopted to banish war and to bring in finally the
reign of universal and permanent peace, must be
one in which every nation can heartily join, and in
which no one, not even the least of them, shall feel
that it has been forced against its will.

These are the great lessons which the history of
the peace movement teaches. We shall do well to

lay them all seriously to heart, as we enter upon what we hope is to be the final stage of the greatest movement which ever engaged the thoughts and the activities of men.

RICHARD COBDEN'S INFLUENCE
TOWARD THE PEACE OF
THE WORLD [1]

THE centenary of Richard Cobden's birth, which fell on the third of June, was widely observed in England and to a less extent in this country. Synchronously with the Cobden banquet in London, the American Free Trade League had a dinner in Boston at which the life and work of Cobden were reviewed by Charles Francis Adams, Edward Atkinson and others, and cablegrams were exchanged with the Cobden Club of London. At the Mohonk Arbitration Conference on the same evening Horace White and Edwin D. Mead paid tribute to Cobden's service in behalf of international arbitration and peace.

Apart from any judgment upon his free trade doctrine, Cobden deserves to be held in the highest esteem and veneration by all the friends of international justice and peace because of his extraordinary efforts in behalf of international concord. It is no exaggeration to say that of all the men in public

---

[1] Editorial in *Advocate of Peace*, July, 1904.

life who have up to the present time thrown the weight of their position and talents in favor of international goodwill and pacific settlement of disputes, he was easily first. He was literally the first public man in Europe to bring the subject into political prominence and compel it to remain there. His early peace work was done under peculiar difficulties. It was at the time when Lord Palmerston was at the height of his policy of *taquinerie*, as Bastiat called it, and had half the countries of Europe mad at England. It was at this time that Cobden threw himself into the breach, to counteract the evil influences of the Foreign Secretary, and prevent open rupture with various European states, especially with France.

After the celebration on January 31, 1849, of the overthrow of the corn laws, he turned his activities in the House of Commons toward an attempted reduction of armaments, reduced expenditure and the at that time still more delicate subject of international arbitration. In 1847 he had strenuously though unsuccessfully resisted the attempt made by the government to increase the British forces. Nearly every Liberal paper in the kingdom was against him, but he kept up his opposition to increase of armaments, as bad foreign policy, as long as he lived. On the 5th of January, 1849, he wrote: " It would enable me to die happy if I could feel the satisfaction of having in some degree contributed to the partial disarmament of the world." In 1862, only two years before his death, he made his memorable attack in the House on Palmerston's senseless policy of national defense. The same year he published his pamphlet, " The Three Panics," in which he exposed the groundlessness and absurdity of the alarms of invasion which had seized successive governments in 1848, 1853 and 1862.

All this was pioneer work, and fruitless for the time. But he stated and made clear what the problem was, and the nation has never been able to get the subject out of its consciousness. The Czar of Russia in his famous Manifesto of 1898 was only repeating in a larger way what Cobden had set forth thirty years earlier.

In 1849, June 12, he brought forward his motion in favor of arbitration, the first of its kind in the British Parliament. It was supported by petitions, numerously signed, sent in from all parts of the nation. It was a very moderate proposition. What he proposed was simply the agreement by treaty with other countries to submit disputes for settlement to mixed commissions, with an umpire if necessary. His motion was sneered at as utopian. " The small wits of the House," as he styled them in a private letter, " tittered at the very word arbitration." But nearly half the members left the House rather than vote against the motion. That gave him much satisfaction. Lord Palmerston, in moving the previous question, made a speech full of admissions, and seventy-nine members voted with Cobden. That was a beginning — a great beginning under the circumstances. It was only twenty-four years afterwards that a similar motion made by Henry Richard received the votes of half the members, and forty-four years later that the Cremer resolution had not a single vote recorded against it.

Cobden was strongly opposed to the policy of intervention in foreign affairs as both unjust and dangerous, and let no opportunity slip of protesting against it. War loans to foreign governments he also regarded as iniquitous and economically bad. In 1850 he made a powerful speech against the proposed British loan of seven million pounds to Austria. In the following year he denounced still more vigorously, in a public meeting called by himself, a loan of five and a half millions which had been asked for by Russia. It is easy to imagine what he would say to-day, when these loans have become such a conspicuous feature of every conflict that a refusal to make them might easily prevent any war. He would lay the responsibility for present wars heavily upon the international money lenders.

Cobden opposed war on ethical grounds, but nearly all his great arguments against it were drawn from economic and humanitarian considerations. War and preparation for it consumed the resources which were required for the improvement of the temporal condition of the people, and herein too lay much of the wickedness of it. The maxim, "In peace prepare for war," he considered as untenable as ever fell from the lips of man. He opposed with extraordinary and comprehensive insight the whole course of the Palmerstonian Ministry in the Crimean War — standing with Bright almost alone in opposition to that insane conflict, which had driven the whole nation out of its senses.

Cobden doubted if constitutional freedom could co-exist with large standing armies, history showing no instance where they had flourished together. If he were living now, the " bloated armaments " of our time would find no more stout and persistent adversary than he, and his own England and our America would be arraigned by him for their naval folly in this direction with that relentless logic of common sense with which he handled every question that he touched.

The civilized world has come up to Cobden, and even gone beyond him, in the matter of arbitration. In the matter of non-intervention in the quarrels of other countries, it has made great progress. It has advanced far in the improvement of maritime law, which he so forcibly urged, and in freer international intercourse. It will yet come round to all his anti-war and anti-militaristic positions, which were founded deep and strong in both the moral and material interests of the people of all countries.

WHITTIER, THE POET OF PEACE[1]

> " ' Hate hath no harm for love,' so ran the song;
>   ' And   peace   unweaponed   conquers   every
>   wrong! ' "

WHITTIER was the poet of peace, because, more than any other American, he was the poet of moral force. He never wrote for art's sake, as Longfellow and Bayard Taylor did; nor for simple amusement, as Holmes often wrote; nor to embellish some philosophic thought, like Emerson; nor to surprise and stun, as Lowell seems sometimes to have done. His pen was always tipped with moral principles — not the abstract principles of ethics, but the live, warm principles of ordinary human life, with its sufferings, its rights and its possible high destinies. Here, in men, everything with him centred. No one ever had a deeper, clearer conception of the intrinsic value of men, nor of the sacredness and inviolability of their persons and their rights. This made him the unalterable foe of everything that injured men or sacrificed their liberties. Thus his fine poetic gift, which revelled among the stars

---

[1] Two-minute address at the unveiling of the Whittier tablet in the Hall of Fame, New York, on May 30, 1907.

and delighted itself in the fascinations of nature, was turned to the support of everything that blesses, and against everything that curses.

He opposed war for the same reason that he opposed slavery, because of its horrors, its cruelties, its injustices, and the base and ignoble passions which it usually springs out of, or, at any rate, always arouses. As he would not have held a slave for any earthly consideration, so he would not have gone to war and killed, or caused the killing of men, to save a race from slavery or even a nation from dismemberment, so loyal was he to duty as he conceived it. To have done so would have been, for him, to sacrifice the most binding and cherished moral principles that inspired and guided his life. His patriotism — and none ever had a finer and nobler love of country — had therefore to proceed in other ways than those marked by bloodshed and destruction.

He not only held war to be always wrong, but he also held moral principles — truth — to be the unfailing and speediest weapons for the overthrow of iniquity and the establishment of justice, if they were only faithfully used. Thus he sang of peace as the greatest glory of man, and of " the Light, and Truth, and Love of Heaven " as the weapons divinely appointed for the conquest of the world.

In " The Peace Convention at Brussels," in " Disarmament," in the " Christmas Carmen," and

in lines and stanzas here and there in many other
poems, this marvellous poet of Moral Force, of the
conquering power of Truth and Love, bids us

". . . grasp the weapons He has given,
    The Light, and Truth, and Love of Heaven ";

bids us

" Sing out the war-vulture and sing in the dove ";

bids us

" Lift in Christ's name his Cross against the
        Sword ";

and inspires our hope and courage in the great
" war against war," which is now everywhere on,
with the sublime prophecy of " The Peace Convention at Brussels," when

" Evil shall cease and Violence pass away,
    And the tired world breathe free through a long
        Sabbath day."

TO JOHN G. WHITTIER [1]

Herald of life and truth;
　　Prophet of peace and love;
Strong as the eagle's youth;
　　Tender as voice of dove.

Trumpet blast comes no more;
　　Toil of the race is done;
Rest by the quiet shore,
　　Watch till the setting sun.

Light-beams from heaven's Sun
　　Break through the mists of death;
Comes to thee His " well done "
　　Sweet on the zephyr's breath.

---

[1] Written before Whittier's death and published in the *Advocate of Peace*, August, 1892.

THE COMING OF PEACE

A Christmas Meditation [1]

Kant's famous essay on " Eternal Peace " was, in name at least, suggested by a satirical picture of a graveyard painted on the coat of arms of a Dutch innkeeper, and bearing the legend " To Eternal Peace." This droll combination of ideas in a cheap picture suggested a noble line of thought to the mind of the great philosopher, and so the great essay came into existence one hundred years ago. It does not at first sight look as if the graveyard of international hatreds were as yet at all crowded, or were likely soon to be. Was Kant right? Or are hate and war to be eternal?

What was the state of things when the Christmas song of peace and goodwill was first sung? If one of the shepherds of Bethlehem, or one of the wise men from the East, had been asked what the angels meant by saying, " On earth peace, goodwill toward men," his brain would have been much puzzled over the question. Some simple notion of peace of soul

---

[1] *The Christian Register*, December 26, 1896; *Advocate of Peace*, January, 1897. By permission.

might have come to him, or of peace between a few individuals. The shepherd might have said that it meant the relief of Israel from his oppressors. But peace on earth, as we think of it — how could this simple child be supposed to have any possible relation to such a thing? Was it conceivable that the awful tyranny of arms then everywhere enthroned could be thrown down? None of those who came about the infant Jesus could even have proposed to their minds such a problem. Peace on earth, goodwill to men! Was it merely a piece of angelic mockery from the skies?

The condition of the world at that time has often been called one of peace — by what right I do not know. Milton has put the thought into his " Ode on the Nativity." But why was " no war nor battle sound heard the world around? " Why were the doors of the temple of Janus shut? Simply because one great, brutal power had its iron foot on the neck of all the rest. The sword was sheathed only because there were no more heads on which to use it. There were no more nations to subdue. All were down at the feet of Rome. If you could have looked into the hearts of the peoples who had been robbed of their liberties, where anger and revenge forever blazed, you would have said that the condition was anything but peace, that the awful slaughters would soon enact themselves again. There can be no peace where love is dead, where justice and liberty are trampled under foot. It was a black, angry, hopeless sky in which the angels sang their song of peace and goodwill.

Christianity is the religion of peace, because it is the religion of love and justice. Even in Kant's time, only one hundred years ago, it seemed as if it had proved a failure in both these aspects. The world never seemed more out of joint. " Eternal Peace " was written in 1795, during the brief " Peace of Basle," the first lull in that frightful storm of communism, aggression, wrath and carnage which swept over Europe from 1789 to 1815. Kant's pen was scarcely dry when the storm burst again, with added fury. Eighteen hundred years had passed since Christianity first uttered its message of peace and goodwill. During this long period it had preached its principles of righteousness, love, benevolence, and brotherhood in Western Asia, through all Europe, and for more than a hundred years in the New World. Every winter the Christmas story had been told; every spring that of the resurrection. In a way this teaching had exercised an enormous influence, as every student of history knows. A number of evils it had driven out of human society — gladiatorial shows, polygamy, slavery, private war. It had made multitudes of homes happy in the peace of God. It had in consid-

erable measure created peace among individuals in
their local relations, and even among groups of
individuals near to each other or widely separated.
But upon national walls of separation it had had no
appreciable effect. Nations were still considered one
another's natural enemies, proper subjects for subju-
gation and humiliation. Only a very few times
before Kant had any one ventured to suggest the
possibility of international peace. War between nations had been condemned as inhuman and unchristian by only a handful of Christians. By most,
hatred of other nations was considered a Christian
virtue, and war against them the most glorious of
callings.

With the century which opened with Kant's
" Eternal Peace," an entirely new order of events
began, in both social and international relations,
the fruit, of course, of all the seed sown previously.
The chief general characteristic of the hundred
years now closing has been the ceaseless struggle of
the new order to supplant the old. The old has
maintained itself so vigorously that many still believe
that no progress has been made toward the eradica-
tion of the spirit of hatred and war and the establishment of goodwill and peace. Many of the
bloodiest wars known to history have been waged in
this century. Nearly five millions of soldiers are now
under arms. More than fifteen millions more have

been trained, and are ready to fall upon each other at any moment. The nations of Europe spend annually two-thirds of their income in preparing for war and paying the interest on their war debts. These debts have accumulated with frightful rapidity during the last quarter of a century, until at present they aggregate nearly thirty thousand millions of dollars. Implements of war were never so numerous nor so deadly as now. With their huge armies, their great fleets, their troublesome budgets, their hatreds and jealousies, the nations are constantly in a state of feverish dread and anxiety. Last winter, in Congress, a representative stood up in his place and declared solemnly that, though eighteen Christian centuries have passed, yet no progress had been made toward the reign of peace and goodwill, using this argument to urge our country at once to militarize itself after the fashion of Europe.

Is militarism ultimately to overrun the world and kill out forever the spirit of love and goodwill? If there were not facts of another order, it would seem so; and the angels' song of peace might well grow silent. The new order of facts, indicating that the era of peace and goodwill, for men and nations, is not far away, may be thus briefly summarized:

1. The sense of justice, the disposition to treat one's fellow-men in a way that is right and fair, has grown remarkably and become widely prevalent

since the century began. This sentiment has manifested itself not only in individual acts of social righteousness, but also in improved laws and customs. Righteousness is the foundation of peace.

2. Equally marked has been the expansion of the spirit of benevolence. The disposition and the purpose to do one's fellow-men good have prevailed in an entirely new way. A new and momentous fact has been the permanent organization, for world-wide service, of religious and philanthropic work. Into this channel now flow millions of money from millions of loving hands. Love in united service is the creator of peace.

3. Universal education, with its humanizing influences, had its origin in this same expanded spirit. Science has had a new birth, and has contributed greatly to the improvement of human life. Education and science are cosmopolitan. They know no race, nor national boundary, nor prejudice. They are the messengers of peace.

4. Liberty and free government have made great strides. Slavery and the slave trade have practically disappeared. Before Kant's time popular government had had hardly an experimental existence. Now all the nations of the Western World are independent republics. Two republics have become permanent in Europe. The other European nations, with one or two exceptions, have developed consti-

tutional methods until they are essentially governments of the people. Liberty is the handmaid of
peace, and free governments will not long endure
militarism.

5. Increased commerce and travel, growing out
of the general spirit of the century, have brought
peoples into contact, made them acquainted, removed prejudices, created common interests, modified laws, internationalized capital, opened world-
wide opportunities for labor. Commerce and travel
demand peace.

6. The socialist labor movement, which originated in modern ideas of justice and fairness, and
in the enlarged feeling of brotherhood, is, in its
deeper, durable elements, a profound indication of
the revulsion of modern thought and sentiment
against the unreason and the brutalities of force and
the selfishness which made these dominant. The
union of labor the world over is one of the giants
who are to pull down all the pillars of militarism.
Labor hates war and loves peace.

7. The century has had nothing more expressive
of its characteristic spirit of justice, fairness and
tenderness than the new place which it has given to
woman, in education, in benevolent activities, in
freedom of service. Her advancement is accompanied by a corresponding decline in the supremacy
of the law of might. She is the queen of peace,

which is certain to follow in the footsteps of her elevation.

8. Our century has substituted law for the fist and the revolver, in the settlement of private disputes. The duel, which was in honor everywhere when the century opened, has been outlawed in all but one or two countries calling themselves civilized, and is on the point of outlawry in these.

9. The special philanthropy of peace has been permanently organized. Beginning in 1815, peace societies have been established and have grown in number and influence until their ideas and aims have taken hold of men of all classes, and have made for themselves a permanent place in the press and in literature. Since the Paris Exposition, these societies have held an annual congress in different cities of the world. They have won the respect and coöperation of governments and statesmen. They have their special organs of propaganda, and have created for themselves a central International Bureau at Berne. They are now recognized as a permanent feature of modern humanitarian activity. They are powerfully aided in their work by that unique, eminently practical association in Europe known as the Interparliamentary Peace Union, having now a membership of more than twelve hundred statesmen, coming from every European Parliament. Special arbitration conferences, like that at

Washington in April last, and the annual conference at Lake Mohonk, have greatly strengthened the movement.

10. The growing peace sentiment has also expressed itself in the numerous international arbitrations of the last hundred years. Before Kant's time there had been nothing really deserving such a name. Since then, there have been nearly a hundred important cases, involving every sort of international dispute, participated in at one time or another by nearly all the governments of the world. The year just closing, which began with serious international disturbance, has been remarkable for this class of settlements, or arrangements for settlement. Chief of these has been the Venezuela case, but there have been no less than six others touching the relations of ten different nations. No dispute now arises between civilized nations without the question of arbitration being raised in connection with it. No fact could be more significant.

The movement for the permanent legislative recognition of the principle of arbitration has begun already to culminate. Cobden, at the instigation of the peace societies, started it in 1849. Henry Richard and Charles Sumner followed it up in the seventies. It has since made its way into many parliaments. Several treaties have already been made between some of the smaller nations, agreeing to refer all questions in difference to arbitration. Switzerland has treaties of this kind with France, Ecuador, and San Salvador. Spain and Honduras have one. Belgium has like treaties with Venezuela, the Orange Free State, and Hawaii. More significant still, the two great English-speaking nations, which have many years been discussing the subject, are, as the recent message of President Cleveland declares, just about to enter into a general treaty of this kind, creating at the same time a court of arbitration as permanent as the treaty itself.

The momentum of these great movements of our time has become at last irresistible. The old order of hate and violence must give way before the growing might of love and reason. Disarmament must soon take place by a process of natural decay, if it does not come amid the desolations of a social and international cataclysm which the tyranny of militarism is inviting. " War is on its last legs." Eternal peace is the early destiny of humanity. The angels' song of peace and goodwill this Christmas may well seem more than prophecy.

WILLIAM PENN AND THE GOSPEL
OF THE INNER LIGHT [1]

————————

THE gospel of the Inner Light, the doctrine that God makes himself known directly to the souls of men everywhere and in all ages, was the final and highest word of the Puritan Reformation. It originated in a great, epoch-making spiritual experience, or group of spiritual experiences, in an age when life had largely departed from the established religious forms and spiritual darkness was heavy upon the people.

The principle had lain from the beginning enfolded in Christian teaching, and in all true Christian life, but without enunciation and interpretation. Indeed, it had lain at the heart of everything that deserved to be called religion, from the beginning of human thought about the invisible Author of the universe and of human reverence and worship. Serious men had always felt, and in measure realized, that God appeared to them within, however much, from custom and association, they tried to

————

[1] A " Thursday Lecture " in the First Church in Boston, 1903. By permission, from *Pioneers of Religious Liberty in America*, Boston, American Unitarian Association, 1903.

discover, or did discover, him without. But this truth, like every great truth, became a gospel of power for the liberation and enlargement of men's lives only when it was articulately set forth by persons who had mastered its secret.

From the theological point of view the principle sprang as a corollary from the primary truth of the universal and impartial love of God as Father of the human race, which the early Friends vigorously maintained against the stiff and heartless predestinarianism of the time. Love is light, they saw and felt. The God who loved all men must of necessity communicate himself to the souls of all. The True Light, which came into the world as the supreme revelation of the character of God, must light every man, in measure, in all ages and all times. The historic manifestation was only the revelation in a special and superlative way of a process coeval with human society. Thus the first promulgators of the gospel of the Inner Light supported by simple but unanswerable theological judgments what they had realized in their own experience to be true.

It would be most interesting and instructive to examine critically the relations of the doctrine of the Inner Light to the historic Christ, to the conscience and to the general philosophy of the Christian religion; but the purposes and limits of this address do not permit the entrance of this field.

We are to study to-day the part which this truth has played in the establishment and development of religious liberty.

The first effect of a clear perception of the fact that God communicates himself directly to all human souls is a sense of the place and value of the individual personality. He to whom God speaks, whom God deems worthy to receive his direct messages, must have a high intrinsic worth, must be, potentially at least, a king by divine right within the domain of his own being. He must be his own priest, offer up his own sacrifices, do his own worshipping. However much he may resort to others for instruction and help, he must in the last appeal be his own interpreter of what he is to believe and follow.

Just here is found the primal secret of religious liberty, indeed of all liberty. Out of this experience of inner connection and communion with the Highest comes to all serious souls self-respect before God and man, the exaltation and supremacy of conscience, the purpose to realize one's own place and destiny, a fine sense of obligation to a life of godliness and manliness. The soul that realizes this high prerogative can admit of no lordship of men over it. It is to God alone that it bows in reverent and loving submission, and says, " Thy will be done." With the self-respect and the devotion to righteousness come courage and endurance in the face of persecution and suffering, if these have to be met.

This secret of liberty and of earnest, patient, heroic effort for its attainment has been the common possession of all the prophets and martyrs of freedom, though realized less clearly and fully by some than by others. It inspired, directed and upheld the Pilgrims and, in somewhat less measure, the Puritans, as well as the Friends, both in the Old World and in the New, in their great moral struggle for liberty of self-directed worship. It was the guiding star of John Robinson, of William Brewster, of Thomas Hooker, and of Roger Williams, no less than of George Fox and of William Penn, though it did not lead them all equally far.

But the principle of the direct light of God in the human soul, the spiritual side of the now generally accepted doctrine of the divine immanence, had a still deeper effect upon the minds of those who felt the fullness of its power. It created intelligent, large-minded respect for others — a much greater thing than self-respect — and much more productive of freedom in its wider social and political aspects. Self-respect is not a very difficult accomplishment for thoughtful and sincere men: it grows with small nurture directly out of the elemental instincts of self-preservation and self-expression. Respect for others, sincere and abiding, without which there can be no social liberty, is the most difficult of spiritual attainments.

It was just here that the doctrine of the Inner Light produced one of its finest fruits. If God reveals himself to the souls of other men besides one's self, in however dim a way, then these other men have the stamp of worthiness put upon them by the Most High himself. Whom God respects and treats in this high way as he treats me, I must respect as I respect myself. Whom God has cleansed I must not call common. I must leave him free to think, to respond to God in his own way. I must not put him into any spiritual bonds, for thereby I shall exalt myself above God and dishonor Him from whom my own light comes.

Respect for others which is born of this source knows no limit. Men may differ with me in thought as widely as the poles are apart: I shall still respect them. I shall uphold for them the liberty to think, and to speak as they think, as I claim these prerogatives for myself. They may be wicked and unworthy, and I may feel myself bound in duty to try to bring them back to the path of goodness; but even thus I shall employ only the high art of persuasion and reproof by truth and love, and not the low art of compulsion by brute force and persecution. They may be my enemies, bitter and injurious; but even so I shall refuse to lower myself to hate and harm and enslave them, because of the common relation which they and I hold to God.

The Friends of the seventeenth century carried this principle of respect for others, so deeply involved in the principle of the Inner Light, to its logical conclusion. They granted to others without regard to creed what they claimed for themselves. Herein they differed from all other types of the Puritans, with rare exceptions, and went beyond all other leaders of the Reformation up to their time. The Puritans in general, in spite of the great stress which they laid upon the Bible as the supreme standard of faith and practice, believed in the direct communication of God with the soul — at any rate, with their own souls. But they did not go far enough to see the wider aspects of this truth. The self-respect in which the principle issues they felt strongly, and were ready to undergo all sacrifices to attain personal liberty and liberty for those who believed as they did. But of genuine religious respect for others, for those of pronouncedly different religious conceptions, they knew little. They were not only not willing to undergo sacrifices and sufferings for the sake of the liberty of other sectaries to think and speak as they thought, but they undertook, where they had the power, to compel by force conformity to their own tenets. They became persecutors, and did men and women to death for insisting on the same liberty of religious thought, interpretation and statement which they had suffered all manner of hardship to obtain for themselves.

The promulgators of the gospel of the Inner Light not only conceded liberty of thought and speech to others: they suffered and died for the spiritual rights and liberties of those of other beliefs as they did for their own. They never persecuted, or showed the least spirit of persecution, even when they had the power, as in the colonies of Pennsylvania and West Jersey. They did not retaliate against those who had maltreated them and sent many of their choicest members to prison and to death. They thus won for themselves and for humanity, on this high ground, one of the greatest victories of liberty — many think the greatest — ever gained, and left incorporated in our civilization — let us hope for all time — what is a commonplace to-day, namely, the principle of respect for the personalities, the intellectual and spiritual liberties, of other men than one's self. So accustomed are we in this day to enjoy this priceless boon that it is difficult for us to credit the fact that at least one person died in prison for it every month during the entire reign of Charles I.

But the gospel of the Inner Light carried its

apostles one final step further. They saw that the sharers in the directly communicated light of God were thereby treated as members of a common family. That is what gave the doctrine of universal brotherhood so profound a meaning to them, and made them its unwavering exponents and defenders when it had no other friends. Brotherhood, in their conception, was not a mere sentimental correlate of the Fatherhood of God, held as a philosophic theory. Its basis was deeper also than the likenesses everywhere observed among men and their dependence upon one another. Beyond all these grounds for treating their fellow-men as brethren they saw God himself conducting himself as a father toward them, as well as toward themselves, and doing this in the deepest and truest way. They saw him holding communion with them, enlightening, instructing, inspiring, guiding, supporting, comforting, as well as reproving and disciplining them with a father's faithfulness, patience, and wisdom. The brotherhood of men was thus to them a practical divine kinship, founded in the active Fatherhood of God, to be cherished as sacredly as the relationships between the members of a true family.

The Friends were thus carried by their gospel of Inward Light into the most active manifestations of the spirit of brotherhood, the effort to bring men to the realization of a life essentially divine, the uplifting of the down-trodden, the deliverance of those in bondage, the amelioration of the lot of prisoners and other unfortunates, universal religious liberty, the endeavor to secure for all equality of rights before the law. It was their practice of brotherhood, when they were persecuted as well as when they were left in the enjoyment of their rights, not their theories about it, that made their work from the middle to the close of the seventeenth century probably the greatest and most wide-reaching contribution to religious and civil liberty ever yet made. Only those who practise brotherhood can long hold any true theory of it or really promote it. These men filled the world with their doctrine of the ideal brotherhood of man, and by their practice of what they preached made it seem something more than the baseless fabric of a dream.

Of this group of men who made the gospel of the Inner Light a permanent part of all subsequent religious thought, the most conspicuous in the practical application of its principles to social and political problems was William Penn, the stateliest, shapeliest, manliest figure of the second half of the seventeenth century, a man now always placed in the list of the few really great men of history.

Penn came upon the scene at a very critical time in the history of the development of religious free-

dom. The great wave of the Puritan Reformation
had practically spent itself. All the prominent Puritan leaders — William Brewster, John Robinson,
John Winthrop, John Cotton, Thomas Hooker,
John Hampden, John Pym, John Milton, Oliver
Cromwell, Sir Harry Vane — were gone. Roger
Williams, the only other colonial leader, with the
possible exception of Thomas Hooker, who went as
far as William Penn in his advocacy of religious
liberty, was worn out and dying. The Royalist
party, with its high-handed monarchical proclivities
and its unblushing corruptions, had been restored;
and Charles II. and then his brother James dictated
from the throne — or attempted to dictate — both
the politics and the religion of the nation. Algernon
Sidney had been banished, and was living in exile
in Rome. It was the period of the infamous Jeffreys
and his Bloody Assize. The party of pure religion
and of popular rights, though strong among the
masses, was for the time being submerged. Puri-
tanism itself was degenerating into a hard-and-fast
ecclesiasticism, and in its strife for political as well
as religious ascendancy was losing much of its original spirit and becoming intensely bigoted and intolerant. In New England it had only been saved
from moral shipwreck at the hands of the clergy-
men and the magistrates by the influence of Roger

Williams and his friends, and by the heroic treatment of a group of followers of the Inner Light, the remarkable voyage of whose " Mayflower," the " Woodhouse," is only less famous than that of the ship of the Pilgrims, because it was not the first to be made. The severe persecution of these men and women and the final martyrdom of a number of them created a reaction among the people, and ultimately restored to Massachusetts the spirit which had planted Plymouth Colony.

There is nothing in the whole scope of religious biography more interesting than the manner in which William Penn became a spiritually free man, an experience through which one must have passed himself before he can do anything effective for the freedom of others. Nearly everything in his inheritance and home surroundings was of a nature to make him the pliant slave of circumstances. No man was ever less so. What he heard in the Puritan atmosphere at the school at Wanstead about civil liberty and the rights of Parliament doubtless had much influence with him, but it is entirely inadequate to account for the course which he took. That can only be explained as the result of the work of God within him. Born a Royalist, of a father who was a heavy drinker and a glutton, as well as a man of rough military life and habits,

Penn had, on the one hand, a restless, impetuous, combative disposition, fond of dress and pleasure, ready to run the common course dictated by custom and self-interest. On the other hand, he was characterized by a thoughtful, contemplative, sincere, pure-minded, richly religious nature, on which the light of God fell as the rain and sunshine upon a deep, fertile soil.

The struggle in him between the earthy and the spiritual began at the early age of twelve and lasted for nearly a dozen years. He had at this age, while alone in his room, what he always believed to be a special visitation of God's spirit, which awakened all that was best in him, inspired and comforted him, made him feel that God was in direct communication with him, and that he was called to a holy life. The conflict through which he passed till his twenty-third year was a very trying one. At Oxford, where he studied for three years, he was fined and then expelled from his college because he preferred Quaker meetings to the regular church services, and, as report has it, joined the Puritan students in tearing off the surplices from the Royalist boys. He was sent to France later, to cure him of his deepening religious tendencies. The court of Louis XIV., at which he was introduced, was then at the height of its brilliancy. Under the influence of the court and its surroundings he fell away from his best light into a life of pleasure and vanity, though never, he assures us, into impurity, profanity, or even vulgarity of speech.

Returning home a well-educated and polished young gentleman, well versed in theology — which he had read at Saumur under the distinguished Moses Amyrault — his father set him to study law at Lincoln's Inn; but, observing during the time of the great plague that his son was turning again to a serious life, he put him into business and military positions, which, he thought, would prevent any return of his former religious ideas. But these were living in him, and had silently developed during his stay abroad.

At the age of twenty-three another special call came to him through the preaching of Thomas Loe, a Friend whom he had heard at Oxford. This time his final decision was made, and he was henceforth a son of the Inner Light and a free man. His father protested, entreated, stormed, whipped him, beat him, turned him out of doors. But it was all in vain. Young Penn, with his face toward the sun, stood his ground, and entered at once upon that consecrated, divinely guided, earnest, steadfast, patient, benevolent life, which was to be so fruitful in the promotion of both religious and civil liberty to the people of his own and of subsequent times.

Penn's spiritual freedom, it may be remarked in

passing, was of that rare kind which avoids asceticism and austerity, on the one hand, and every form of impurity and looseness, on the other. He relished, as occasion offered, all the lawful pleasures of life; but the corrupt, obscene, and disgustingly low manners and habits of people in high places, among whom he was so often cast at court and elsewhere, made not the least inroad upon the purity and loftiness of his soul. He walked in the light of God; and that light kept him clean and strong, and therefore free.

The fruit of the principles which had mastered his soul began at once to manifest itself. During the next fifteen years, which he spent in preaching the new gospel and suffering for it, his work for religious freedom was as constant, brave and effective as was ever done in England. His high social standing and friendly connection with the royal family put him into a position of extraordinary influence; and this, though often exposing him to suspicion and vituperation, he never failed to use in behalf of the liberties of all his fellow-citizens, without regard to creed. He became, because of the unequalled depth and breadth of his conceptions, his impartial and incessant efforts and the faithfulness with which he used his position of commanding influence, the foremost of the seventeenth-century apostles of religious liberty.

When imprisoned himself, as he was several times, Penn addressed powerful appeals for liberty of conscience and civil freedom to those in authority. When out of prison, he did the same for others, Catholics as well as Protestants. In his letter to the Earl of Orrery, Lord President of Munster, on the occasion of his first imprisonment, he touched the great springs of all his future efforts for liberty — the inalienable rights of conscience, the principles of English liberty as set forth in the Great Charter, and the evil effects to the State of religious intolerance. Imprisoned in the Tower for nine weary months on a charge of blasphemy, because he had in one of his books criticised the crude tri-theism of the time, when told that the Bishop of London had determined that he should recant or die a prisoner, he replied: " My prison shall be my grave before I will budge a jot, for I owe my conscience to no mortal man. I have no need to fear: God will make amends for all. They are mistaken in me. I value not their threats and resolutions; for they shall know I can weary out their malice and peevishness, and in me shall they behold a resolution above fear, conscience above cruelty, and a baffle put to all their designs by the spirit of patience. . . . A hair of my head shall not fall without the providence of my Father that is over all." He did not budge a jot, nor did he die in prison, nor did a hair of his head fall.

The trial of William Penn and William Mead in 1670, while the Conventicle Act was in force, for speaking at a meeting in Grace Church Street, when they had been locked out of their own house of worship, was one of the most memorable in English history. It took place eighteen years before the famous trial of the seven bishops, described so graphically by Macaulay's brilliant pen. The victory for justice in which it resulted was also greater than that in the case of the bishops, because the matter at stake was not, as in the latter, a mere question of supremacy between Protestant and Catholic, but the wider and deeper question of general religious toleration and universal civil rights against lawless bigotry and tyranny.

The trial was held at the Old Bailey. Penn's defence, which he conducted himself without counsel, was that the Conventicle Act, which he did not deny that he had broken, was in violation of the principles of the Great Charter. His knowledge of the law enabled him to take advantage of the errors and falsehoods of the indictment, which included the charge of taking part in a tumultuous and disorderly assembly. In spite of the most shameless attempts of the court to silence him, he stood his ground, and made a masterly defence of himself and companion.

When the jury brought in the verdict, " Guilty

of speaking in Grace Church Street," the magistrates were furious, and ordered a new verdict. The jurymen went out, and immediately returned with the same verdict. It was again rejected by the court. Time after time, though brutally threatened and maltreated, these brave men came back with the same judgment. Two days and nights they were kept without bed or food or even water. When they came in for the last time, they had changed the mock verdict into a real one, " Not guilty." The magistrates were dumb with anger and amazement. The crowd in the court-room broke forth into excited demonstrations of approval. In their fury the magistrates fined both the prisoners and the jury for contempt of court. Penn strode forward to the bench, and in the name of the fundamental laws of England demanded his liberty in accordance with the verdict. It was denied him. Refusing to pay their fines, they were all committed to Newgate. The jury, following Penn's advice, brought suit against the mayor and recorder for false imprisonment. They carried the case to the Court of Common Pleas, and won. The judges declared unanimously that a jury had absolute freedom in rendering its verdict. It was a great victory for simple truth and justice, and did much to strengthen the foundations of the growing structure of English constitutional liberty.

Penn's written protests against religious persecution and pleas for civil and religious liberty were numerous, and among the most noble and effective in the whole history of English reform. They were in homely, unpolished Anglo-Saxon English; but they struck hard, and went straight to the heart of the matters dealt with. Memorials to the High Court of Parliament, to the sheriffs of London, to justices and lords; his speeches before a committee of Parliament, and before King James on presenting an address of the Friends; his treatise on "The Great Case of Liberty of Conscience," in which he musters an array of historic example and precedent that reminds one of John Milton; his "Address to the Protestants of All Persuasions"; his tractate on "England's Present Interest"; his "Project for the Good of England"; his political manifesto on "England's Great Interest in the Choice of a New Parliament," in which he set forth the principles, fundamental for all time, in accordance with which the franchise should be used by free and honorable men — all these are papers and treatises which, though in the antiquated language of the seventeenth century, might still be read with great profit, particularly in the none too saintly circles of modern politics. There are no two documents in all English political literature fuller of political wisdom than "The Great Case of Liberty of

Conscience " and " England's Present Interest Considered."

Penn is usually supposed to have been a man of placid disposition, submitting passively to injustice, and never using vigorous and pungent speech in defence of justice and liberty. He was nothing of the sort. He refused from principle to use any physical violence, and was as absolutely master of his spirit as any man who ever trod upon English soil. But " in deeds of daring rectitude " he was unsurpassed. His discarding of the weapons of brute force made him all the more bold and aggressive in the use of those of moral cast, as was the case with our leading anti-slavery reformers. None ever wielded the weapons of truth in defensive speech and in protest against wrong, where occasion demanded, with more naked directness and unsparing keenness than he. He knew not the meaning of fear. He was swift in offence wherever a stronghold of injustice towered before him.

In the trial at the Old Bailey, when the court was browbeating the jury, he exclaimed in manly indignation: " It is intolerable that my jury should be thus menaced! Is this according to the fundamental law? Are they not my proper judges by the Great Charter of England? What hope is there of ever having justice done, when juries are threatened and their verdicts rejected? " When the recorder

maliciously ordered him taken away, declaring that
for such men as he something like the Spanish Inquisition ought to be established in England, Penn
replied: "I can never urge the fundamental laws of
England but you cry, 'Take him away, take him
away.' But 'tis no wonder, since the Spanish Inquisition hath so great a place in the recorder's heart.
God Almighty, who is just, will judge you all for
these things." Chided by Cavaliers for abandoning
the society of gentlemen and associating with the
despised Quakers, who were from among the common people, Penn's moral sense flashed back the
retort: "I confess I have made it my choice to
relinquish the company of those who are ingeniously
wicked, to converse with those who are more hon-
estly simple." In a letter to the vice-chancellor of
Oxford University, by whom students inclined to
Quakerism were treated with great contempt and
severity, he wrote: "Shall the multiplied oppressions
which thou continuest to heap upon innocent English people for their peaceable religious meetings pass
unregarded by the eternal God? Dost thou think to
escape his fierce wrath and dreadful vengeance for
thy ungodly and illegal persecution of his poor children? I tell thee, no. Petter were it for thee thou
hadst never been born. Poor mushroom, wilt thou
war against the Lord, and lift up thyself in battle
against the Almighty?" In the "Great Case of

Liberty of Conscience," written while he was a prisoner in the Tower as a political suspect, he declares that in trying to secure uniformity in religious belief " the way of force makes instead of an honest dissenter but an hypocritical conformist, than whom nothing is more detestable to God and man." In " England's Present Interest Considered," a tractate inspired by the purest and loftiest patriotism, he utters a protest of rare power against the abuses and cruelties practised throughout the nation in the effort to bring about religious conformity, and pleads for toleration as the surest means of putting an end to the prevailing confusion and disorder. " Your endeavors for uniformity," he says, " have been many: your acts, not a few to enforce it. But the consequence, whether you intended it or no, through the barbarous practices of those that have had their execution, hath been the spoiling of several thousands of the free-born people of this kingdom of their unforfeited rights. Persons have been flung into gaols, gates and trunks broken open, goods distrained, till a stool hath not been left to sit down on; flocks of cattle driven off, whole barns full of corn seized, threshed, and carried away; parents left without their children, children without their parents, both without subsistence. But that which aggravates the cruelty is the widow's mite hath not escaped their hands: they have made her ' cow the forfeiture of her conscience,' not leaving her a bed to lie on nor a blanket to cover her. And, which is yet more barbarous, and helps to make up this tragedy, 'the poor helpless orphan's milk, boiling over the fire, has been flung to the dogs, and the skillet made part of their prize.'"

The severest ordeal through which Penn had to pass in his work for religious liberty was that which befell him in his advocacy of toleration for Catholics as well as Protestants. The torture of soul which he experienced in this conflict, wherein for twenty years he was misrepresented and maligned as a scheming Catholic, a Jesuit, a hireling of the pope, was tenfold greater than any suffering which vile imprisonment or bodily abuse caused him. In these latter he gloried, in a high, triumphant spirit. He gave hard blows, and he knew how to take them. But to be treated as a consummate liar, an arch deceiver, a snake in the grass, cut his fine, sensitive, honorable soul to the very quick, and sometimes wrung from him expressions of a grief too keen and overmastering to be concealed. But he never flinched from the trying duty until he had done his work. Pleading before a committee of Parliament his case and that of his co-religionists under persecution as Papists, he said:

"That which giveth me a more than ordinary right to speak at this time and in this place is the great abuse that I have received above any other of my profession; for of a long time I have not only been supposed a Papist, but a Seminary, a Jesuit, an Emissary of Rome. . . . What with one thing and what with another, we have been as the wool-sacks and common whipping-stock of the king-dom. All laws have been let loose upon us, as if the design were not to reform, but to destroy us, and that not for what we are, but for what we are not. It is hard that we must thus bear the stripes of an-other interest and be their proxy in punishment. . . . I would not be mistaken. I am far from thinking it fit that Papists should be whipt for their consciences, because I exclaim against the injustice of whipping Quakers for Papists. No; for, though the hand pre-tended to be lifted against them hath (I know not by what discretion) lit heavy upon us, and we com-plain, yet we do not mean that any should take a fresh aim at them, or that they must come in our room; for we must give the liberty we ask, and cannot be false to our principles, though it were to relieve ourselves; for we have good-will to all men, and would have none suffer for a truly sober and conscientious dissent on any hand."

More pathetic and, if possible, more noble still is his language in reply to an urgent request from a particular friend to vindicate himself in a public statement against the calumnies which fell upon him from all sides on account of his frequent visits to James II. in behalf of universal toleration. I quote a few sentences from this remarkable but little known letter:

"I am not only no Jesuit, but no Papist. And, which is more, I never had any temptation upon me to be it, either from doubts in my own mind about the way I profess, or from the discourses or writings of any of that religion. And, in the presence of Almighty God, I do declare that the King never did once, directly or indirectly, attack me or tempt me upon that subject, the many years that I have had the advantage of a free access to him; so unjust as well as sordidly false are all those stories of the town. . . . I have almost continually had one business or other there for our Friends, whom I ever served with a steady solicitation, through all times, since I was of their communion. I had also a great many personal good offices to do, upon a principle of charity, for people of all persuasions, thinking it a duty to improve the little interest I had for the good of those that needed it, especially the poor. . . .

"I am not without my apprehensions of the cause of this behavior towards me, . . . I mean my constant zeal for an impartial liberty of conscience.

But if that be it, the cause is too good to be in pain about. I ever understood that to be the natural right of all men, and that he that had a religion without it, his religion was none of his own. For what is not the religion of a man's choice is the religion of him that imposes it. So that liberty of conscience is the first step to have a religion. . . . If, therefore, an universal charity, if the asserting an impartial liberty of conscience, if doing to others as one would be done by, and an open avowing and steady practising of these things, in all times, to all parties, will justly lay a man under the reflection of being a Jesuit, or a Papist of any rank, I must not only submit to the character, but embrace it, too; and I care not who knows that I can wear it with more pleasure than it is possible for them with any justice to give it me. For these are corner-stones and principles with me; and I am scandalized at all buildings that have them not for their foundations. For religion itself is an empty name without them, a whited wall, a painted sepulchre, no life or virtue to the soul, no good or example to one's neighbor. Let us not flatter ourselves. ' We can never be the better for our religion, if our neighbor be the worse for it.' . . .

" He that suffers his difference with his neighbor about the other world to carry him beyond the line of moderation in this, is the worse for his opinion, even though it be true."

This noble vindication, unsurpassed by anything in the language, ought to have silenced the tongue of calumny forever; but it did not. He was still hounded by enemies and arrested and brought to trial no less than three times afterward, until he was finally cleared of all blame by King William himself and by the King's Bench at Westminster.

This work of Penn in England for liberty of conscience, for universal religious toleration, and the equal and impartial rights of all before the common law, has been less heralded and less appreciated than his experiment in the New World. It ought not to have been so. The two were only different parts of the same service to the cause of liberty. What he did in England produced the training and laid the foundations for the American experiment, and was by all odds the more difficult and trying. What he did on the banks of the Delaware was simply to test in practice, with a comparatively free hand, the soundness and practicability of the doctrines whose advocacy had cost him so many years of thankless labor, social ostracism and relentless persecution on his native soil. It took, of course, a political genius of the highest order to conceive and execute the American scheme. But it required, in addition to genius, a sustained moral heroism, unsurpassed in the annals of reform, to maintain for so many years the hard conflict by which he wrested from the English courts and government the recognition, for himself and for multitudes of others, of the simple rights of citizenship and of religion, a victory whose benefits went to all English-speaking peoples.

It would be gratuitous to rehearse before a cultivated American audience the story of the founding and development of the colony of Pennsylvania, and of its extraordinary success, without soldier or armed policeman, for two whole generations of men. Nothing in the annals of the country is better known than this singular romance of our political history, more marvellous in its simple reality than any ideal republic of philosophy or any utopia of political dreaming.

Leaving aside, as not relevant to the purpose of this address, the phase of the experiment which has been most dwelt upon, that of the entire disuse of deadly weapons, it is difficult to say which of the other parts of it — the policy of justice and brotherhood toward the Indians, that of universal religious toleration, and that of equality of rights in the government — was the most successful and the most influential in its ultimate effects on the nation after the colonial period was over.

The Indian policy, which was incomparably successful during the seventy years that it was continued, was finally abandoned by the colony, along with that of the disuse of arms. But it remained as an appealing ideal to the nation during more than "a century of dishonor," with its frightful Indian wars and enormous cost to the country. At last the government, weary of the bitter and costly fruits of the method of oppression and slaughter, found itself practically compelled, by considerations of self-interest and economy as well as of right, to adopt toward the Indians who remained what was substantially the policy of Penn. The results have again justified the method. Since the adoption of the peace policy under President Grant, Indian wars have ceased. The Indians are rapidly becoming civilized, and are being absorbed into the general population and life of the nation. Through it all Penn's influence has been beyond calculation, and it will continue to be mighty until the last Indian remaining becomes a citizen and enjoys all the rights and liberties of his white brother.

The policy of universal religious toleration — a better word than toleration ought to be used to describe it — that was adopted by the founder of Pennsylvania was immensely successful. Though tried for the first time in its full scope — the experiment of Roger Williams having been not only

much more limited, but much marred and broken
by interference from abroad — it worked just as
Penn had often declared in England that it would
work. People of every nation, tongue and creed of
Western Europe flocked to the banks of the Delaware. They lived in mutual respect and harmony,
and the colony grew and prospered beyond all the
others. The effect of this bold, thorough-going and
measurably unhampered experiment in freedom of
conscience and of religious polity was deep and
wide-spread among all the colonial settlements. The
policy finally worked its way, strengthened of course
from many other sources, into the larger life of the
nation, and became part and parcel of the controlling spirit of the American people, as we know it
to-day.

Before leaving England, Penn drew up " The
Fundamental Constitution of Pennsylvania," and
also a " frame of government," as he styled it, for
the ordering of the new colony, in which it was
decreed that " the people themselves were to be the
authors of their own laws in a properly constituted
assembly." Scarcely had he set foot upon the new
soil when he put the frame of government into
operation, calling a general assembly of the farmers
and cave-dwellers on the lower reaches of the
Delaware Bay. In this curious assembly of " plain
people " — very plain people we should think them

— the constitution was adopted and suitable laws passed. For serene audacity and unlimited faith in the undertaking there is nothing of its kind like this in history. Untamed regions, wild Indians, motley groups of settlers, only loosely related, traducers at home, all counted for nothing as obstacles. The thing was of God, and it must go. And go it did, because it was of God. The constitution worked, worked admirably, as any good thing will work when in good hands; and Penn had successfully planted what he had already prophesied in England God would make the "seed of a nation."

This frame of government, though revised and altered in its details, remained essentially unchanged in its principles from the time when its author landed in 1682 until the Revolution of 1776, nearly a hundred years. When the thirteen colonies after the war consolidated themselves into a nation and undertook the difficult task of creating for themselves a constitution, their representatives assembling for the purpose on the very ground where Penn had tried his "holy experiment," this "frame of government," drawn on the other side of the water, furnished, more than any other document unless it be Hooker's Constitution of Connecticut, the fundamental principles for the construction of the new instrument. It is scarcely too much to say that, when the natural history of the American Constitution is fully written, it will be found to have been born, not in the brain of Madison, Hamilton, or Franklin, or of any other of the distinguished statesmen who sat in the Constitutional Convention of 1787 and worked out with so much wisdom the details of our great national charter, but in the brain of this man of God, who in obedience to the heavenly visions that came to him dared to break with all the customs and precedents of his time, and to go as far as his English citizenship and dependence on the crown would permit him to go in creating a government of the people by and for themselves.

The statue of William Penn above the city hall in Philadelphia yonder, which one can easily imagine to blush with shame as certain politicians of the place pass beneath it, is higher from the ground than any other in the world. It is fitting that it should be so. Most men are soon left behind by the march of progress, and their ideals are outgrown when their age has passed away. Not so with Penn. The civilized world, even our own America, has not yet come up with him. He had his weaknesses and his imperfections, especially in his judgments of men; but they were like the spots on the sun; they sprang from the same virtues and energies which made him great and powerful. His central ideals were as eternal as those of the Master, after whom he framed his life and policies, and can never be outgrown. He is still the statesman of the future; and there is no voice out of our country's great past to which the present, with its aspirations, its hopes, its ambitions, its wanderings, its lapses from the high ideals which it had set for itself, might give heed with greater profit than to his.

INDEX

Date Due